Journeys through God's Word

An Introductory Course:
ACTS

Study Guide

John Scharlemann

Edited by Thomas J. Doyle

This publication is available in braille and in large print for the visually impaired. Write to the Library for the Blind, 1333 S. Kirkwood Rd., St. Louis, MO 63122-7295; or call 1-800-433-3954.

Scripture quotations are taken from the HOLY BIBLE: NEW INTERNATIONAL VERSION®. NIV®. Copyright © 1973, 1978, 1984 by International Bible Society. Used by permission of Zondervan Publishing House. All rights reserved.

Copyright © 1999 Concordia Publishing House
3558 South Jefferson Avenue, St. Louis, MO 63118-3968
Manufactured in the United States of America

All rights reserved. No part of this publication may be reproduced, stored in a retrieval system, or transmitted, in any form or by any means, electronic, mechanical, photocopying, recording, or otherwise, without the prior written permission of Concordia Publishing House.

1 2 3 4 5 6 7 8 9 10   08 07 06 05 04 03 02 01 00 99

Contents

Introduction		4
1	Pentecost: The Beginning of the Church	7
2	And the Church Grows!	16
3	The First Martyr	25
4	Out of Jerusalem and into the World	34
5	Peter's Ministry	43
6	Paul's First Missionary Journey	52
7	The Jerusalem Council and Paul's Second Missionary Journey	60
8	On the Road Again	68
9	The Third Missionary Journey Comes to a Difficult End	77
10	The Trials Begin	85
11	The Trials Continue	93
12	Sailing to Rome	100
Glossary		108

Introduction

The study of the Bible is nothing less than an exploration into the thoughts and desires of God for ordinary people like you and me. It takes us from this hardened and selfish world into the promise of a world where God's peace, justice, and mercy will be complete.

Delving into the Bible for the first time can be somewhat intimidating. We are taken to a distant past that is full of unfamiliar customs and traditions. We must become acquainted with a nation that viewed the world differently than many people do today. And we must begin to alter some of our current definitions to grasp the full meaning of our Lord's love and compassion.

As foreign as many customs and traditions might seem to us today, we will discover that people's natures remain the same. We are trapped today—as people were centuries ago—in an imperfect world where evil and pain seem all too prevalent. We, too, can view the world as meaningless and without hope. But Jesus Christ came to rescue the world from its quagmire, and His deliverance continues to change our lives. Pray that the Word of God, as it comes, will begin to alter your perspective. May His promises give you rich and lasting hope and joy!

How to Use This Study

The Study Guide will direct your study of Acts. The typical session is divided into five parts:

1. Approaching This Study
2. An Overview
3. Working with the Text
4. Applying the Message
5. Taking the Message Home

"Approaching This Study" is intended to whet the reader's appetite for the topics at hand. It leads participants into the world of the New Testament while summarizing the issues to be examined. "An Overview" summarizes the textual material used in each session. Before the text is examined in detail, it is viewed as a whole, allowing participants to "see the forest" before "exploring the trees." "Working with the Text" draws participants into deeper biblical study, encouraging them to discover the gems of universal truth that lie in the details of God's Word. When questions appear difficult or unclear, the Leaders Guide provides a doorway to the answers. "Applying the Message" leads participants from the recorded Word of God to its possible application in our present lives. It helps participants more fully realize the implications of God's Word for the daily experience of a Christian. Finally, "Taking the Message Home" invites participants to continue their scriptural meditation at home. Suggestions are given for personal reflection, for preview of the following session, and for private study of topics raised by the session. The study of God's Word will be greatly enhanced by those actively pursuing the suggestions offered in this section.

Each session includes some trivia that is intended to spark interest and generate additional discussion. This can be used to develop inquisitiveness and enthusiasm about related issues ripe for exploration.

A glossary is provided at the end of the Study Guide. Because a study of the Bible will lead participants to language that may occasionally seem foreign and difficult, the glossary will make participants more comfortable with unfamiliar terms, phrases, and customs. The glossary will help them understand biblical concepts such as love and grace, whose definitions may differ from current definitions.

Session 1

Pentecost: The Beginning of the Church

Acts 1–2

Approaching This Study

The New Testament consists of three major types of written material. The four gospels of Matthew, Mark, Luke, and John record the ministry of Jesus Christ. Most of the other books of the New Testament are actually letters written by some of Jesus' disciples. But the Book of Acts is different from these. Although the physician, Luke, writes Acts as a continuation of his historical gospel, the material that he covers in Acts is unique from every other New Testament book. The Book of Acts records what happened to the followers of Christ after His ascension. It describes the birth of the Christian church and the spread of Christianity throughout the Roman Empire. Although its focus begins with the 11 apostles who remained after the death of Judas, it quickly evolves into a record of Paul's missionary journeys through the Gentile lands outside of Palestine. As such, it emphasizes God's gift of grace moving from the Jews to the Gentiles. In the beginning of the book, Jesus tells His disciples, "You will receive power when the Holy Spirit comes on you; and you will be My witnesses in Jerusalem, and in all Judea and Samaria, and to the ends of the earth"(Acts 1:8). The Book of Acts records this sequential spread of the Christian church from its origins at Pentecost in Jerusalem to Paul's witness in the capital city of the Roman Empire. Throughout the book, the presence and work of the Holy Spirit is emphasized. Because the book leads to Paul's trial in Rome, but never describes the events and outcome of that trial, many believe the book was written as a defense for Paul. Whatever its ultimate purpose, the book is a priceless glimpse into the manner in which the Holy Spirit equipped and strengthened the early Christians to bring the Gospel message of salvation and grace through Jesus Christ to the world. It provides us with insights into how the church carried out Christ's Great

Commission to go into all the world, making disciples of all nations by baptizing people in the name of the triune God and teaching them to obey everything Jesus commanded (Matthew 28:19–20), which is, of course, only the beginning of the story. The story of the church continues in the work of Christ's followers today. The work of faithful believers today comprises the latest chapter and the continuing saga of the Book of Acts.

An Overview

Unit Reading

Have a volunteer read aloud Luke 24:36–53. Then have another volunteer read Acts 1 and another Acts 2:1–13; and, finally, have another volunteer read to the end of the chapter.

The Message in Brief

The beginning of the Book of Acts overlaps the ascension account recorded in the Gospel of Luke. In Acts, however, the author emphasizes Jesus' command for His disciples to wait in Jerusalem for the coming of the Holy Spirit. As they wait, they select another individual to replace the position of twelfth apostle vacated by Judas as a result of his suicide. By relying on God's guidance, they cast lots and chose Matthias. Ten days after Jesus' ascension into heaven, the disciples receive the Holy Spirit in a spectacular fashion. The Spirit arrives in a gust of wind and in the presence of tongues of fire, which rest on the apostles' heads. The apostles are empowered to preach God's Word in the various languages of the world. And they are emboldened to courageously proclaim the life, death, and resurrection of Jesus Christ. Consequently, many people convert to Christianity. As evidence of the Spirit's power among them, the Christians live in harmony, daily worshiping the Lord.

Working with the Text

Jesus' Ascension (Acts 1:1–11)

1. Turn to Luke 1:1–4. What was Luke's purpose for writing an account of Jesus' ministry? To whom was the Gospel of Luke addressed? Now, what does the author of Acts suggest about the Book of Acts? Is it a story unto itself or the continuation of a narrative? Again, to whom is it addressed?

2. What important information does Acts 1:3–4 give us about Jesus' post-resurrection appearances? For example, how do His appearances discredit the possibility that the resurrection story was the result of a mass hallucination? How do they undermine the theory that the resurrection story was only the product of someone's invention? How does Jesus' appearance at the dinner table refute the theory that Jesus' resurrection was only spiritual and not physical?

3. Before His ascension into heaven, Jesus promised the disciples they would soon receive a wonderful gift. What would that gift be? Jesus had spoken of this before. Turn to John 14:16–18 and describe Jesus' promise to His disciples before His death.

4. The promise of the Spirit caused the disciples to wonder whether a new age was about to begin. What did they believe would happen at the dawning of the new age according to 1:6? How did Jesus attempt to focus their attention on the real purpose of His kingdom in verse 8?

5. What promise is given by the two angels about Jesus' return? How had Jesus already given this promise to His disciples (Matthew 16:27)?

A Replacement for Judas (Acts 1:12–26)

1. How many believers were present in Jerusalem with the 11 disciples after Jesus' ascension? What had happened to the twelfth disciple, Judas?

2. Peter viewed Judas's death as the fulfillment of two scriptural prophecies. Perhaps the most intriguing of the two quotations points to the need to fill Judas's position with another individual (Psalm 109:8). But read all of Psalm 109. How can you view this entire psalm as an expression of Jesus' experience as He approached His death on the cross? Focus on verses 6–20 and explain how these passages could relate to Judas.

3. What were the requirements for anyone who would fill Judas's position as the twelfth apostle? In what manner did the other apostles finally choose Judas's replacement?

Pentecost (Acts 2)

1. Pentecost was a Jewish festival, which occurred 50 days after the Sabbath of Passover week. It was sometimes called the Feast of Weeks or the Feast of Harvest. This one-day festival would usually occur at the end of May or beginning of June, celebrating the close of the harvest season. Describe the three ways by which the Spirit marked His arrival among the apostles.

2. Peter, empowered by the Spirit, viewed the Pentecost miracle as a fulfillment of prophecy. He quoted from the prophet Joel, who had foretold the beginning of the "last days" hundreds of years before the birth of Christ. What does this suggest about the time in which we live? How might we describe the period of time from Pentecost until now?

3. How would you describe Peter's message to his audience? On what did he focus and why? How did the people respond to his message? Before Pentecost, there were more than 120 believers. How many were added to the faith on this spectacular day?

4. Describe the unique fellowship that existed in the earliest days of the Christian church (Acts 2:42–47).

Applying the Message

1. After the crowd in Jerusalem heard Peter's sermon, they were "cut to the heart." They asked Peter how they should respond to the message of Jesus' death and resurrection. He called upon them to repent and be baptized "in the name of Jesus Christ for the forgiveness of sins." The Greek preposition here indicates purpose; in other words, the purpose of Holy Baptism is to bring the forgiveness of sins. Some Christian denominations view Baptism as a simple rite of naming or christening a child. Why is Baptism much more than that? How does this understanding help us interpret Titus 3:5; 1 Peter 3:21–22; and Acts 22:16?

2. There are some Christians who claim to speak in tongues today. They utter sounds and syllables that arise from an unknown language. But how does such tongue-speaking differ from the miraculous tongue-speaking of Pentecost? What effect do you think this miracle had on those who heard the Gospel preached in their native languages? How did the Spirit use this gift to expand the early church? Now consider 1 Corinthians 14:6–19. How does Paul view the gift of speaking in tongues when no one can understand the language? What does this suggest to you about the priority of speaking in tongues?

3. When Jesus promised He would send His Spirit to the disciples, what did He promise the Spirit would do for them (Acts 1:8)? Many Christians have difficulty sharing their faith with others. They feel intimidated or fearful about uttering the wrong words. What remedy does God offer for this timidity? How important is it to be strengthened in God's Word through which the Holy Spirit works to strengthen our faith?

Taking the Message Home

Review

When Christians worship God, they recognize the existence of three persons in one God—Father, Son, and Holy Spirit. Even though they exist as one God, we often ascribe somewhat different attributes and functions to each person. God the Father is predominantly associated with creation, while Jesus Christ is associated with redemption. After reading Acts 1 and 2 again, how would you begin to describe the role of the Holy Spirit?

Looking Ahead

As time permits, read Acts 3:5–16. List the ways in which you see God's justice and mercy evident in the recorded events. In what manner does this section of Acts influence your view of the Holy Spirit's work?

Working Ahead

Complete one or more of the following before the next session:

1. Ask your pastor about his perspective on tithing in your congregation. How could tithing better enable your congregation to accomplish its task to spread the Gospel?

2. It is a popular belief that all people who are sincere about their religion will find their eternal reward in heaven. Whether people are Jewish, Hindu, Buddhist, or Islamic, as long as they genuinely follow the tenets of their religion, they will be saved. Why do you think this opinion has become so widely held today? What do you think the Christian response should be and why?

3. Reflect on the ideal sermon. What themes do you think a preacher should regularly communicate to a congregation and why? Be prepared to share your thoughts with others in the group.

Did You Know That . . . ?

In some ways, God's people began to come full circle at the Pentecost miracle. Many years earlier, the world's sins had caused a breakdown in communication. After Noah's flood, as the population of the world grew and became increasingly wicked, many arrogant people decided they would build a tower to heaven. In their mad and sinful delusion, they believed they could create a human monument that would span the distance between God and them. God punished these wicked people by confusing their speech. Each began speaking a different language and no one could understand anyone else (Genesis 11:1–9). The doomed monument became known as the Tower of Babel.

Of course, no physical apparatus can bridge the gap between God and people. The schism arose as a consequence of sin and can only be bridged through spiritual healing. That is why Jesus died for the sins of the world. By doing so, He became the link between God and people. So, after Jesus' resurrection, it was no surprise that His Spirit should mend the damage created by the Tower of Babel. Rather than struggle with a confusing host of languages, each person in Jerusalem heard the disciples preaching the Gospel in his or her own language. What had become confusing was now understood. Even as Jesus had died for sin, so the anarchy of sin was being transformed into unity and order. A new age had indeed begun!

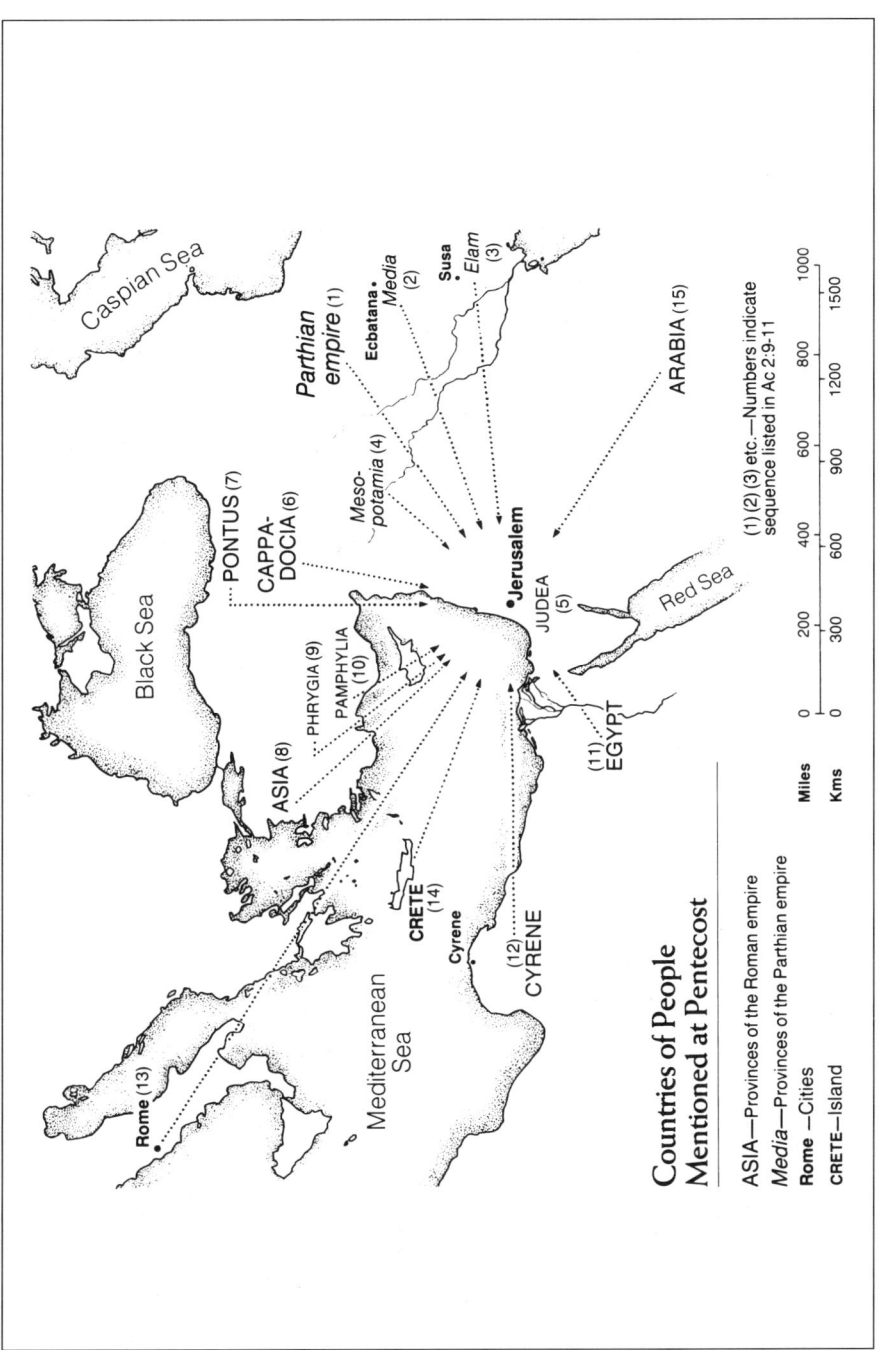

Taken from **NIV STUDY BIBLE.** Copyright © 1986 by The Zondervan Corporation. Used by permission of Zondervan Publishing House.

Session 2

And the Church Grows!

Acts 3:1–5:16

Approaching This Study

One of the remarkable aspects of the early Christian church was its ongoing miraculous manifestations of the Holy Spirit. The Holy Spirit working in the early church enabled the early Christians to witness boldly the Gospel message and to heal in the name of Jesus. The apostles no longer hesitated. They preached courageously and without fear of death. And they accompanied their bold preaching with miraculous deeds. The combination was irresistible. Converts to Christianity multiplied throughout Jerusalem.

Peter and John demonstrated the Holy Spirit's power by their words and in their deeds. Not only did they courageously accuse the Jews of murdering God's Son, but they also emphasized the Good News that Jesus' death achieved full payment for people's sins. And as they preached, they healed. Their presence threatened the ruling religious authorities of Jerusalem, particularly those who had been instrumental in arranging Jesus' death. By word and deed, the apostles gained the hearts and minds of Jerusalem. For those who viewed Jesus' disciples as enemies, the situation became increasingly intolerable. Persecution of the Christians was inevitable. But the Spirit's power was unstoppable. The apostles' work was so impressive, people would bring their sick and injured to rest in the apostles' shadows, hoping this subtle proximity to the Spirit's power would evoke a miracle. What an extraordinary time it was!

Yet sin remained a destructive influence in the world and the church. Even as the early Christians enjoyed unprecedented fellowship and community, two people attempted to cheat God. Ananias and Sapphira committed the first recorded sin within the New Testament church and paid for the transgression with their lives. The wages of sin remained death, even as the free gift of God remained eternal life in Christ Jesus the Lord (Romans 6:23).

An Overview

Unit Reading

Break these chapters into sections, each to be read by a different volunteer. One volunteer should read the story of the crippled beggar (Acts 3:1–10). Let another volunteer read Peter's address (Acts 3:11–26). A third volunteer should narrate the growing resistance to the apostles' work (Acts 4:1–31). As you continue to enjoy the help of volunteers, someone should read the description of the tremendous fellowship experienced by the early church recorded in Acts 4:32–37. Consider having someone with a deep voice read the story of Ananias and Sapphira in Acts 5:1–11. The same individual who read Acts 4:32–37 could complete the reading of Acts 5:12–16.

The Message in Brief

In the middle of the afternoon, in the presence of the citizens of Jerusalem who hustle by the temple, Peter and John heal a beggar who has been crippled from birth. This is an attention-grabber! Peter uses the impact of this miracle to proclaim the death and resurrection of Jesus Christ. As a result of the apostles' message and miracles, the religious rulers of Jerusalem become threatened and contemplate how to silence the apostles. In response, the apostles are empowered to preach Jesus' message of repentance, forgiveness, and grace. Their bold witness of faith inspires other believers in Jerusalem, and the church grows numerically and spiritually.

The destructive presence of sin is unavoidable, however. A married couple by the name of Ananias and Sapphira attempt to cheat the early church out of the proceeds of their land, which they have generously promised to donate. Because their sin is a serious threat to the work and fellowship of the early church, God strikes the couple dead. After this fearsome display of justice, the church continues to grow and teach the Word of God even as it heals the sick and cares for the poor.

Working with the Text

Healing the Crippled Man (Acts 3:1–10)

1. In the previous chapter of Acts, Luke writes that "many wonders and miraculous signs were done by the apostles" (Acts 2:43). Now, as we begin the third chapter of Acts, we witness one such example. Peter and

John, two of Jesus' closest disciples, arrive at the temple in Jerusalem during the middle of the afternoon. They meet a crippled man begging. How long had he been crippled, and how did he get to the temple to beg for money? In whose name was the crippled man healed? Did the crippled man have any kind of faith in Jesus when he was healed (see v. 16)? How old was the crippled beggar (Acts 4:22)?

2. How did the crippled man respond to his healing? What particular part of his feet seemed strengthened? How did he demonstrate his enthusiasm for God, who had healed him? How did those who had known him for many years respond to his healing?

Peter's Homily (Acts 3:11–26)

1. Did Peter accept praise for the healing? Whom did he glorify instead? How did Peter convince the amazed crowd of their sin? But how did he make them aware of a remedy for their guilt and sin?

2. How can we determine that Peter's homily was specifically addressed to the Jews of Jerusalem and would have possibly puzzled the Gentiles (non-Jews)?

Defending the Faith (Acts 4)

1. Of course, not everyone responded positively to Peter's address.

The priests who were serving at the temple that week, the captain of the guards at the temple, and the Sadducees who did not believe in any kind of resurrection but considered themselves of the priestly line arrested Peter and John and put them in jail. Nevertheless, Peter's address had its effect. How many men (remember, this doesn't include women or children) believed according to Acts 4:4? The next day, Peter and John were brought before the Sanhedrin. The Sanhedrin consisted of the ruling religious authorities in Jerusalem. Whose names from the Sanhedrin are listed? Now look up John 18:12–14. To whom was Jesus brought when He was first arrested? In what way did at least two of these men have a very important interest in keeping the apostles quiet?

2. What gave Peter the courage to respond boldly to the Sanhedrin (v. 8)? Compare Peter's character to that which he possessed before Jesus' death and resurrection (John 18:15–18, 25–27). How had Peter been changed by the Holy Spirit? How was his courage a fulfillment of Jesus' promise given in Acts 1:8? How did Peter's courage impress the Sanhedrin (v. 13)?

3. In what single way is salvation promised according to Acts 4:12? How did the Sanhedrin respond to Peter and John? In other words, what did they command Peter and John to do? How did Peter and John's response demonstrate further courage?

4. Peter and John returned to the other disciples and described their experience before the Sanhedrin. Those who heard Peter and John responded with prayer and praise. Summarize their prayer in your own words. What did the Holy Spirit work in all those who were present with Peter and John?

5. How did the early Christians continue to provide for those in need? Who, in particular, is credited for selling his property so that those in need could be satisfied? Remember his name!

A Taste of Justice (Acts 5:1–16)

1. What was Ananias and Sapphira's sin? When Ananias and Sapphira approached Peter, he immediately knew something was wrong. He realized Satan had influenced their behavior. According to Peter, to whom had they lied? As a result, what happened to Ananias and Sapphira?

2. Now, it might seem at first glance as if Ananias and Sapphira's punishment was particularly severe. Yes, they were deceptive and deceitful, but should they have lost their lives over their attempt to cheat the Lord? First of all, remember that death is the just consequence of sin. Read Genesis 2:15–17 and Romans 6:23 as proof. Every one of us will die because of our sin, no matter how minor our sin may seem. Ananias and Sapphira simply suffered the common fate more immediately. Secondly, this was the first recorded sin in the New Testament church. It was particularly important for God's church to receive correction at its very beginning. Compare this tragic deception with that of the Old Testament villain, Achan (Joshua 6:15–19; 7:1, 20–26). How are God's actions consistent between the Old Testament and the New Testament?

3. Solomon's colonnade was a porch outside the courts of the temple in Jerusalem. Acts 5:12 indicates the Christians commonly met at this location. But this was the Jewish temple! Why weren't they ejected? What does this suggest about the bond between Jews and Christians in the earliest days? Why is this not surprising (Acts 3:22–26)?

4. After witnessing the fate of Ananias and Sapphira, many were reluctant to join the church (Acts 5:13). But that does not mean the church no longer grew. Verse 14 indicates more and more people believed in Jesus and were added to the church. So what kind of individuals do you think were reluctant to join?

Applying the Message

1. After healing the crippled beggar at the temple, Peter preached boldly. He no longer hesitated in accusing his audience of killing "the author of life." This was a powerful accusation! But notice how he followed his condemnation with words of forgiveness and promise in Jesus Christ. In what ways do you think a pastor's sermon would be effective if it resembled Peter's homily, that is, emphasizing sin and grace by condemning people for their violations of God's will but immediately announcing forgiveness and peace with God through the death of Jesus Christ? In what ways does your liturgy or worship format reflect sin and grace? How could you use Peter's technique to evangelize effectively to your friends or neighbors?

2. The fate of Ananias and Sapphira should continue to make all

Christians pause as they contemplate their offerings to the Lord. Who among us has not withheld some of what we could have willingly given to God? Ananias and Sapphira's sin grew more serious when they lied about their giving. In what ways might Christians act in a similarly hypocritical fashion about their obedience to God's will? How is hypocrisy harmful to the church?

3. Americans live in a society that is tolerant toward religion. We can be thankful not many of us have been hauled before the courts to defend our Christian faith. But there are examples of Christians who have felt they must obey God rather than men and have wrestled with the question of disobeying civil law rather than breaking God's will. Can you think of such examples? Do you think you would have the courage to suffer the consequences of breaking the law of the land rather than the Law of God? How does the Holy Spirit provide Peter courage under such circumstances?

Taking the Message Home

Review

Reread this section of Acts. How would you describe the power of the Spirit in the earliest days of the church? In what ways do you think today's church would benefit by such spectacular manifestations of the Spirit?

Looking Ahead

Read Acts 5:17–7:60 and reflect on Stephen's courage. Write a summary of his sermon and bring those notes to the next session.

Working Ahead

Complete one or more of the following before the next session:

1. The apostles of the early church proclaimed the Good News of Jesus Christ. Everywhere they went they spread the message. Have you known anyone who is equally zealous in proclaiming God's Word? In what ways do you think such a bold and tireless proclamation could benefit the church? Might it also cause offense? How and why?

2. As a result of the world's sin, Christians sometimes feel jealous of other brothers and sisters in Christ. Within every congregation some members are wealthier or more gifted than others. How do you think the leaders of a congregation should treat the wealthy and the poor? Should a distinction be made? In the real world, do you think preference is sometimes given to those who have more than others?

3. In our next session we will read about a believer named Stephen who was the first Christian executed for his faith. Imagine if our government suddenly outlawed Christianity. The sentence for known believers would be death. Predict what would happen to the churches of America.

Did You Know That . . . ?

As the Book of Acts progresses, fewer and fewer miracles are recorded. To be sure, evidence of the Spirit's presence and power continues throughout the entire chronicle of the early Christian church, but the dramatic nature of these miracles appears to diminish as time goes by. It is as if the Holy Spirit, having ignited the church through spectacular miracles, increasingly responds less sensationally and with more subtlety. God can and does work in miraculous ways today, but nothing compares to the depth and breadth and authenticity of the miracles performed in the days immediately following Pentecost.

Death of Ananias by Gustave Doré

And Ananias hearing these words fell down, and gave up the ghost ... (Acts 5:5 KJV) from *The Doré Bible Illustrated.* By permission of Dover Publications, Inc.

Session 3

The First Martyr

Acts 5:17–8:1a

Approaching This Study

Oddly enough, the message of forgiveness and grace in Jesus Christ has always threatened various people. We might wonder why this is so. Why should the blessed gift of salvation offered freely through Christ evoke such hostility? One reason is exposed in this session's reading. The Jews believed their salvation depended on pleasing God by following the proper rules and obeying the right regulations. Jewish religious leaders had established comfortable positions by convincing their followers of the necessity of working for salvation. When the Christians claimed that heaven was purely God's gift to people, the Jewish leaders were threatened. And when these same Christians demonstrated the power of their message through miraculous healings, the Jewish leaders panicked. They began persecuting the Christians. Finally, they killed a Christian named Stephen. Now, some might have been concerned that Stephen's death would slow down the rapid growth of the church, but God's Spirit remained in control. Stephen's death and other threats of persecution pushed Christians out of Jerusalem and into the farthest regions of the Roman Empire, where they would continue to convert men, women, and children. This session's story may end in Stephen's tragic death, but we will keep our eyes fixed on God's continuing guidance. Through Stephen's martyrdom, the kingdom of God would travel beyond Jerusalem's city gates, into Judea, Samaria, and the ends of the earth—just as Jesus had promised!

An Overview

Unit Reading

As volunteers read this section from Acts, one brave speaker could assume Stephen's role and stand before the group, reading Acts 7:2–53 as a sermon.

The Message in Brief

As the apostles continue to heal the sick while boldly preaching the Gospel of Jesus Christ, the religious authorities rise up in fear. The apostles are arrested and put in jail, but an angel miraculously frees them and commands them to continue preaching. Furious, the ruling religious authorities (the Sanhedrin) wish to execute the apostles, but a Pharisee named Gamaliel persuades them otherwise. After being persecuted, the apostles are freed. They continue to preach and teach. As the church experiences growing pains, the believers—with the support of the apostles—choose seven men who can assist in administering to the needs of the faithful. One of them, Stephen, boldly preaches about Jesus. Jewish leaders arrest him and falsely accuse him of blasphemy. After Stephen accuses the Sanhedrin of stubborn unbelief, he is dragged from the city and stoned to death. Stephen becomes the first martyr of the Christian church.

Working with the Text

The Persecution of the Apostles (Acts 5:17–42)

1. What was the Sadducees' motivation to arrest the apostles (Acts 5:17)? Who freed the apostles from prison? Now turn to Acts 12:6–10. Who was responsible for Peter's release from prison? Look at Matthew 28:2 and explain who was responsible for rolling the stone away from Jesus' tomb. In these instances, how did the angels fulfill their role as described in Psalm 91:11–12?

2. The Sanhedrin—the Jewish court of religious leaders numbering between 70 and 100 men—were livid. Even though the Sadducees had arrested the apostles, the apostles had gained their freedom and publicly preached and taught once again. When holding court, the Sanhedrin would sit in a semicircle. We can imagine how they looked as the apostles were hauled before them. They questioned why the apostles had disobeyed the command to stop preaching about Jesus. What was Peter's response in Acts 5:29? What is Paul's command to Christians about honoring those in authority (Romans 13:1–7)? How can we combine these two statements into a guiding principle for the Christian's attitude toward governing authorities?

3. Who was Gamaliel? Acts 22:2–3 tells us something interesting about him. What is it? Gamaliel was a wise man. He reflected on history and recalled two other individuals who had disrupted the status quo. One was named Theudas. What did he do and what happened to him and his followers? Another was named Judas the Galilean. What did he do and what happened to his followers? If Jesus had been just another false teacher or zealot, what would have happened to His movement by now? What does that suggest about the validity of the Christian church?

Seven Helpers Chosen (Acts 6:1–15)

1. As idyllic as conditions appeared in the early church, it wasn't long before the consequences of sin disrupted its fellowship and community. Perhaps a considerable length of time lapsed between the end of Acts 5 and the beginning of Acts 6. During that time, the church began including Gentile Christians, specifically of Grecian background and language. And, alas, conflict arose along ethnic lines. The Gentile Christians complained their widows were not being cared for as properly as the widows of the Jewish Christians. How did the apostles solve this problem? As a result of their solution, what happened in the church? In fact, what specific profession experienced a large number of conversions?

2. Stephen was one of the 7 selected to help the apostles, but he wasn't one of the 12. Still, what power was he given through the apostles' laying on of hands (Acts 6:8)? Once again, resistance arose against Stephen's testimony to Jesus Christ. How did Stephen's enemies provoke an uprising against his teachings? In particular, what false accusations did they level at him (Acts 6:14)? How and to whom were these

accusations successfully spoken once before (John 2:19–22; Mark 14:57–59; Mark 3:1–6)?

Stephen's Martyrdom (Acts 7:1–8:1a)

1. Stephen's sermon involves a recounting of Old Testament history and some of the stories that deal with the selection and protection of God's people, Israel. Rather than discuss each story, consider the theme of Stephen's message. How would you describe God's relationship with His people? Throughout Israel's history, God chose individuals upon whom He showered His favor. But how did the people respond to those favored by God? What is Stephen's point in recalling these events according to Acts 7:51–53?

2. What does Stephen say about the temple of Jerusalem (Acts 7:48–50) using Isaiah as his source? Why do you think this would cause an uproar among the Jewish religious leaders?

3. Stephen was aware his words of accusation would provoke lethal anger. But, full of the Holy Spirit, he looked to heaven. Describe what he saw. How did his vision resemble that of Daniel in Daniel 7:9–14? How does Paul support this imagery in Ephesians 1:19b–23?

4. According to the first half of Acts 8:1, who was among the murderers giving approval to Stephen's death? Who was this man (Acts 13:9)?

5. As Stephen lay dying, what were his last words? How does this compare to the death of Jesus (Luke 23:34, 46)?

Applying the Message

1. The apostles experienced a remarkable act of deliverance. After they were imprisoned for proclaiming the Gospel, an angel of the Lord released them. Do you think angels continue to help the faithful? How?

2. It's remarkable to see the apostles' reaction to their persecution before the Sanhedrin. After they were flogged and commanded not to speak about Jesus, they left, rejoicing for the privilege of suffering for their Lord. Then they kept on preaching and teaching. Can you think of an experience when you were scorned or persecuted for your belief in Jesus? How did you feel? How might the joyful attitude displayed by the apostles be an inspiration the next time your witness of faith is rejected or threatened?

3. It is somewhat sad to read about the conflict that arose between the Jewish Christians and Gentile Christians. How do you think the same problem could arise today between ethnic groups within a congregation? Give examples. Now, the easy solution might have been to establish two different churches, one for the Grecian Christians and one

for the Hebraic Christians. Is this the route taken by the disciples? After reading Galatians 3:26–29, why do you think the early apostles may have considered this an unthinkable option? How would you apply the principle established by Paul in Galatians 3 to contemporary congregations?

Taking the Message Home

Review

If possible, read Acts 5:17–8:1a again in its entirety. Focus on the statement given in Acts 5:39 by Gamaliel, "If it is from God, you will not be able to stop these men; you will only find yourselves fighting against God." Reflect on the truth of this statement as demonstrated so far by the events recorded in Acts.

Looking Ahead

Read Acts 8:1b–9:43 before the next session. List the characters who are introduced in this section (excluding Peter and John) and write a brief summary of what they did.

Working Ahead

Complete one or more of the following before the next session:

1. On the road to Damascus, a strict Pharisee named Saul was converted to Christianity. He saw a blinding light and heard the voice of the resurrected Lord calling to him. Saul then changed his name to Paul and became the greatest missionary in the history of the Christian church. We praise God that conversion comes to all of us in an instant by God's grace alone. God continues to save lost souls in the twinkling of an eye. Many people experience this through Baptism as infants, so they have no conscious recollection of the event. Others may experience conversion as adults. If you know of someone who remembers when she or he received the gift of faith in Jesus, ask that individual to share the experience with you.

2. One believer named Philip opened up Scripture to an Ethiopian who was reading from Isaiah 53. Through the power of the Holy Spirit working through God's Word, the Ethiopian became a Christian and was baptized. What does this suggest to you about the importance of learn-

ing and understanding the Bible? In what way will you commit to continued growth in your study of Scripture?

3. Another individual named Simon was amazed at the apostles' power to heal. He was a magician and wanted to pay the disciples for their spectacular spiritual gift. The disciples condemned him because he wanted to use the Spirit's power for his own aggrandizement. How might individuals today use the church for their own interests rather than for the joy of sharing the Gospel of Jesus Christ with others?

Did You Know That . . . ?

The process by which the seven assistants to the apostles were chosen is an interesting one. According to Acts 6:3–5, the whole group of believers chose the seven. In other words, they were elected to their roles. However, once elected, these individuals were commissioned by the apostles; that is, the apostles authorized the seven to carry out their appointed duties. And the commission was sealed and blessed through the laying on of hands (Acts 6:6). When Timothy was ordained into the office of the ministry, a group of elders or pastors commissioned him through the laying on of hands (1 Timothy 4:14). Titus was given the responsibility by Paul to appoint or ordain elders in every town in Crete (Titus 1:5). Paul and Barnabas oversaw the appointment of elders or pastors in the towns where they established churches (Acts 14:23); but, interestingly, the Greek word for these appointments can either mean "to appoint" or "to elect by show of hands." So, although it is somewhat unclear how the early church selected their pastors, they seem to have been chosen by a mixture of election, commissioning or appointing, and the laying on of hands. The Lutheran Church—Missouri Synod retains this mixture when it ordains men into the office of the public ministry. Men are trained at the seminaries and "commissioned," that is, authorized by the seminary as candidates for the office of the ministry after having been examined about their beliefs. Then a congregation elects one of them as their pastor. When the new pastor is ordained, other pastors from the surrounding congregations lay their hands on the individual and so complete the process. Whenever a man is ordained into the office of the public ministry, we see echoes of the early church!

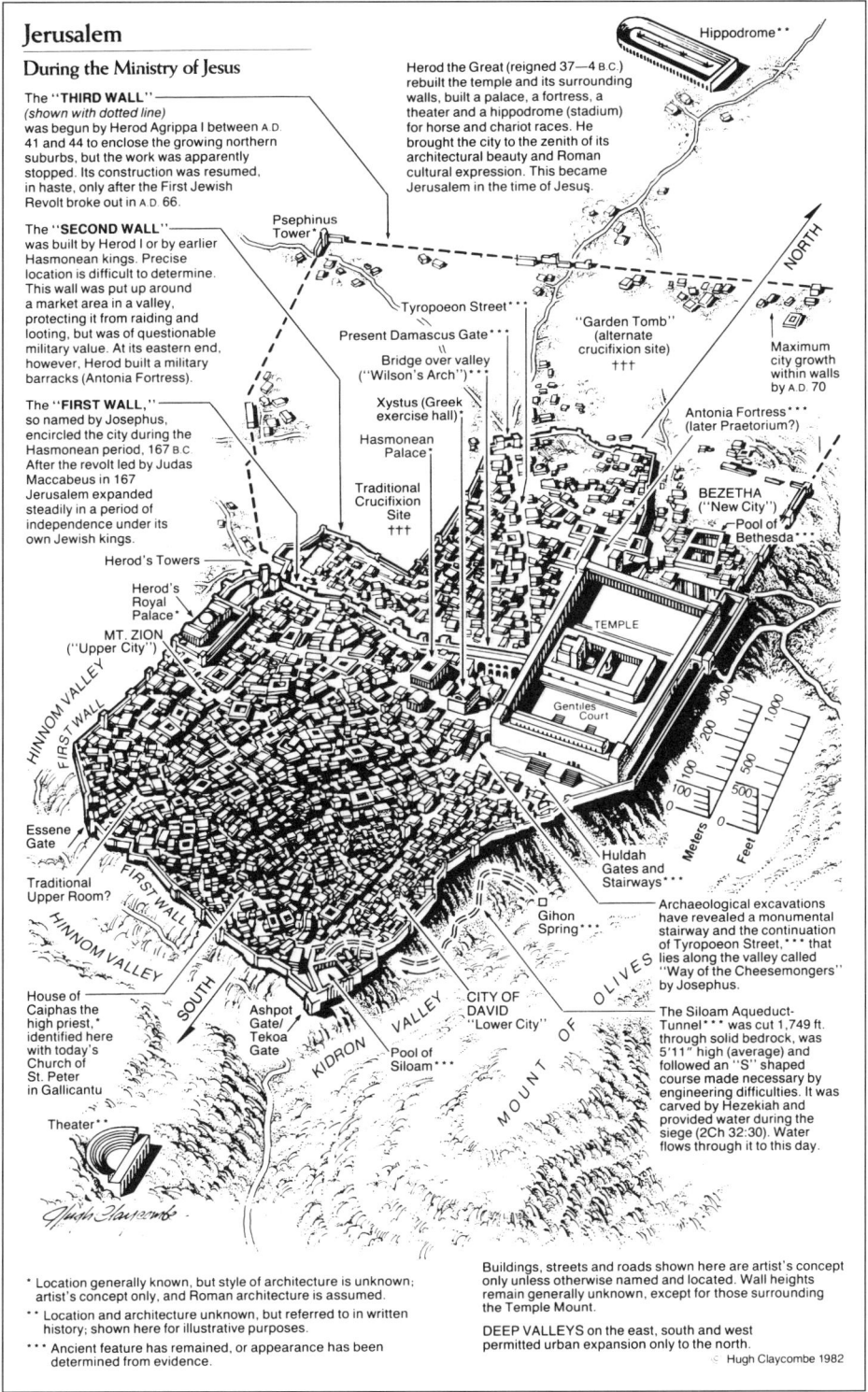

Session 4

Out of Jerusalem and into the World

Acts 8:1b–9:43

Approaching This Study

So far, with some exceptions, the news of Jesus' resurrection had spread no further than the confines of Jerusalem and its nearby villages. But God clearly desired that the saving message of the Gospel spread throughout the world. The Spirit of the Lord had ignited the Christian church. Now the Lord would use the catastrophe of Stephen's death and the subsequent persecution of the church-at-large to initiate an outward movement of the faith. We can only imagine how distressed and discouraged many of the early Christians felt as the persecution grew more widespread. Even though the Lord had warned them of its inevitability, the reality was difficult to endure. Some may have questioned the Lord's providence. But, once again, the Lord transformed the agony of persecution into a blessing. When the leader of the persecution, through the divine intervention of the Lord Jesus, also became a Christian, the persecution eased—but not before God's will had been accomplished. The Christian faith had flowed beyond Jerusalem into the world.

An Overview

Unit Reading

One volunteer may read Acts 8:1b–40. Acts 9:1–19 provides an enjoyable opportunity to assume roles. One person may read the narration, another speak the words of Jesus, and still another the words of Saul. A final reader could speak the words of Ananias. The rest of chapter 9 may be read by another volunteer.

The Message in Brief

As a result of the persecution against the believers led by Saul, many Christians flee Jerusalem to other areas of the region. In this way, the Lord uses an evil offense against His church to force the spread of the Gospel into the world. One individual who leaves Jerusalem is Philip. As Philip preaches in Samaria, a convert and magician named Simon wants to purchase the power of the Holy Spirit. Peter rebukes Simon for his wickedness. God leads Philip to an Ethiopian who desperately wants to understand God's Word found in the Old Testament. After explaining how the prophet Isaiah pointed to Jesus as the Messiah, Philip baptizes the Ethiopian. The resurrected and glorified Jesus finally appears to Saul in a blinding light while he is on his way to persecute Christians in Damascus. As a result of Jesus' appearance, Saul becomes a believer. To the amazement of those who know him, Saul begins preaching the Gospel of Jesus Christ in Damascus. Meanwhile, Peter heals a paralytic named Aeneas and raises a woman named Dorcas from the dead. Through such miracles the Holy Spirit causes the church to grow.

Working with the Text

The Church Is Scattered (Acts 8:1b–25)

1. The Lord transforms disastrous situations into good! After the martyrdom of Stephen, the church went underground. Although the apostles remained in Jerusalem, many Christians fled the city, taking the Gospel of Jesus Christ with them. Who in particular is mentioned as a leader of the persecution? Where did Philip go? How were people prepared to hear the Gospel as a result of miracles Philip performed in Jesus' name?

2. A man named Simon practiced sorcery in Samaria. Look up Leviticus 19:26, 31 and Isaiah 47:12–15. What is God's attitude toward sorcery? What happened to Simon's followers when Philip arrived? What did Simon do when he heard Philip and saw his miracles? Do you believe Simon's conversion was genuine? Why or why not?

3. One of the interesting aspects of this section revolves around the Baptism of the Samaritans. They were baptized into the name of Jesus, but for awhile, no spectacular manifestation of the Holy Spirit was evident. Once Peter and John placed their hands on them, it was clear they had received the Spirit. Read Acts 10:44–46 and 19:6. How did the Spirit manifest His presence in these situations? What did Peter promise would happen to those who were baptized in Acts 2:38? Acts 8:18 suggests something spectacular happened when the Samaritans were baptized. Acts 10:44–46 describes how the Spirit manifested His presence before the Gentiles for the first time. The Gentiles began speaking in tongues and praising God. Then in 19:6, when Paul arrived in Ephesus, the Spirit demonstrated His presence through speaking in tongues and prophesying. This has led some Christian denominations to claim one must receive a second "Baptism of the Holy Spirit"—which requires speaking in tongues—before one is saved. But does speaking in tongues always accompany Baptism in Acts (Acts 2:41; 8:36–39; 9:17–19; 16:13–15; 16:31–34)? Why do you think it was important at various times for the Spirit to appear in such a spectacular fashion (Acts 11:15–18; 15:6–12)? How are people assured of salvation according to Mark 16:16? In other words, must one speak in tongues to be assured of salvation?

Philip Meets the Ethiopian (Acts 8:26–40)

1. Someone has described the Bible as one long story about God's search for His people. Before Philip met the Ethiopian, how can we tell the Lord was already searching for the Ethiopian?

2. The Ethiopian eunuch was reading Isaiah 53:7–8 when Philip arrived. The Ethiopian was curious about the figure being described in the reading. Philip pointed to Jesus. Read Isaiah 52:13–53:12 and list the

various ways in which this passage describes the person and work of Jesus.

3. After the Ethiopian was baptized, what happened to Philip? At the end of the story, where do we leave him? Now turn to Acts 21:8–9. Where is Philip some 20 years later?

Saul Becomes a Believer (Acts 9:1–31)

1. How did Saul feel about Christianity before his conversion (Acts 9:1–2)? What information does Saul provide about his background that explains his hostility toward Christians (Acts 22:2–5; Galatians 1:13–16)?

2. Describe Jesus' confrontation with Saul. What did Saul see and hear? What did his traveling companions experience? The Lord prepared Ananias (not the one who withheld the proceeds of his property from the apostles) to meet Saul and heal him. What was Ananias's reaction to the Lord's call? How did the Lord describe Saul's upcoming ministry (Acts 9:15–16)?

3. How long did it take Saul to start preaching the Gospel once he was a believer (Acts 9:19–20)? What was the natural reaction to his preaching by those who had known him beforehand? Now Paul was on the receiving end of the persecution! How did he escape the martyrdom that was planned for him in Damascus? Even the disciples were scared

of Paul at first. Wouldn't you be? Who defended Paul and where have we heard of him before?

4. According to Acts 9:31, how far had the church spread by this time? Jesus' promise to the apostles in Acts 1:8 was almost fulfilled. To what area had they yet to travel with the Gospel? How do we, Jesus' contemporary disciples, continue to fulfill Jesus' promise?

Two Great Miracles (Acts 9:32–43)

1. When Peter healed Aeneas, to whom did he give credit? How did this spectacular miracle increase the membership of the Christian church?

2. Tabitha was the Aramaic name and Dorcas the Greek name for "gazelle." How does this name seem fitting for her personality as described in Acts 9:36, 39? Now read 1 Kings 17:17–24 and 2 Kings 4:31–37. Also read Acts 20:7–12 and Luke 7:11–17. Over the centuries and through various people, how are God's miracles similar?

Applying the Message

1. Consider Simon the sorcerer's request to purchase the power of the Holy Spirit. What was Peter's response to Simon's request (Acts 8:20–23)? What did this indicate about Simon's spiritual state (Acts 8:23)? How could Simon's motives be seen today?

2. Read again Isaiah 52:13–53:12. In what ways do you think this passage could be particularly effective in sharing Jesus with a Jewish friend or acquaintance?

3. One cannot read about Saul's persecution of the Christians without realizing he was obsessively zealous in his faith. When Saul was defending the Jewish tradition, his zealotry was destructive and sinful. But after conversion, how was this trait transformed and used by the Lord for building His kingdom (2 Corinthians 11:16–33)? Can you share any examples of people with wicked traits who, after receiving the gift of saving faith, used those same traits to serve the Lord?

Taking the Message Home

Review

As time permits, reread Acts 8–9. Count the number of miracles evident in these chapters and share your count with others in your group.

Looking Ahead

Read Acts 10–12 before the next session. These three chapters focus on the ministry of Peter, the same apostle who denied knowing the Lord when Jesus was arrested. Peter was always a rather boisterous man, although streaked with cowardice. In what way do you see the Lord using Peter's outgoing, boisterous nature for the good of His kingdom after God diminishes his cowardly side?

Working Ahead

Complete one or more of the following before the next session:

1. Read Galatians 3:26–29. Should any congregation be divided along racial or economic barriers? Why or why not? Could you describe your own congregation as a good example of "unity in diversity"? In what ways?

2. Do you think it would have been easier to believe in Jesus if you had been an eyewitness to His ministry? Or do you think you might have dismissed Him as a false prophet? Why?

3. As Christians fled persecution in Jerusalem, many of them landed in Antioch. Find the city of Antioch in a Bible atlas. Why do you think Antioch might have been a good launching point for Paul's missionary journey into areas we today call "Turkey" and "Greece"?

Did You Know That . . . ?

So many legends accompany the figures of the New Testament. These legends cannot be considered factual, yet they are interesting to ponder. For example, legend states that Philip became a bishop in the city of Lydia. Simon the sorcerer is said by the historian Justin Martyr to have lived in Rome under the Emperor Claudius while founding a destructive Christian heresy called "Gnosticism." It is unrealistic to link the conversion of the Ethiopian eunuch with the foundation of the Christian church in the area we call Ethiopia today. Nevertheless, when the first known Christian missionaries entered Ethiopia in the fourth century, they found there an early form of the Christian church! Over the centuries bands of Christian women have founded "Dorcas societies," which engage in social services and which are named after the woman who was so loved by the early Christians and resurrected by Peter. Two early church fathers, Eusebius and Origin, state that Peter went to Rome and suffered martyrdom as an old man. He was crucified head downwards during the reign of Nero, probably around A.D. 64. The present St. Peter's Church in Rome is claimed to rest on the site of Peter's tomb!

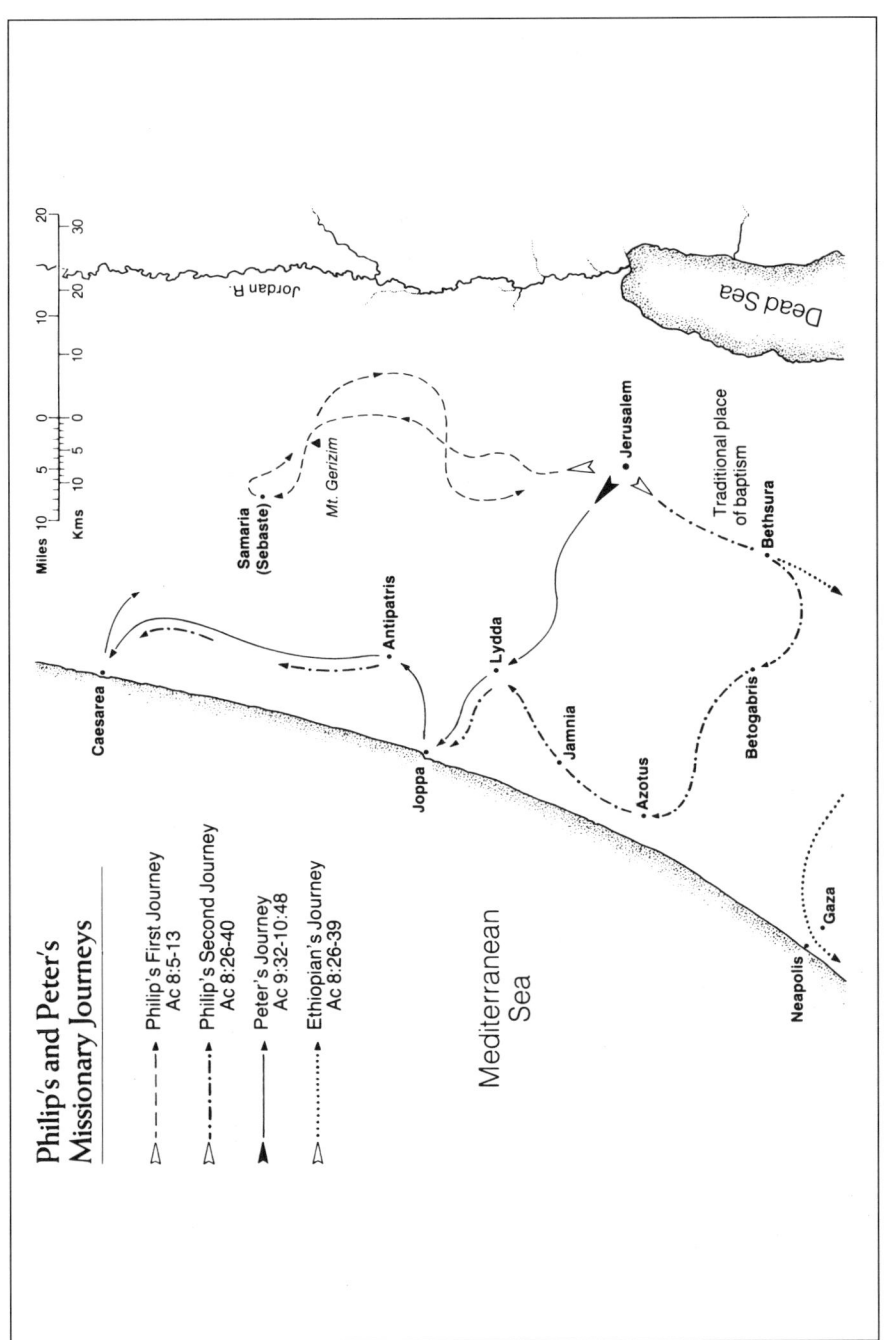

Taken from **NIV STUDY BIBLE**. Copyright © 1986 by The Zondervan Corporation. Used by permission of Zondervan Publishing House.

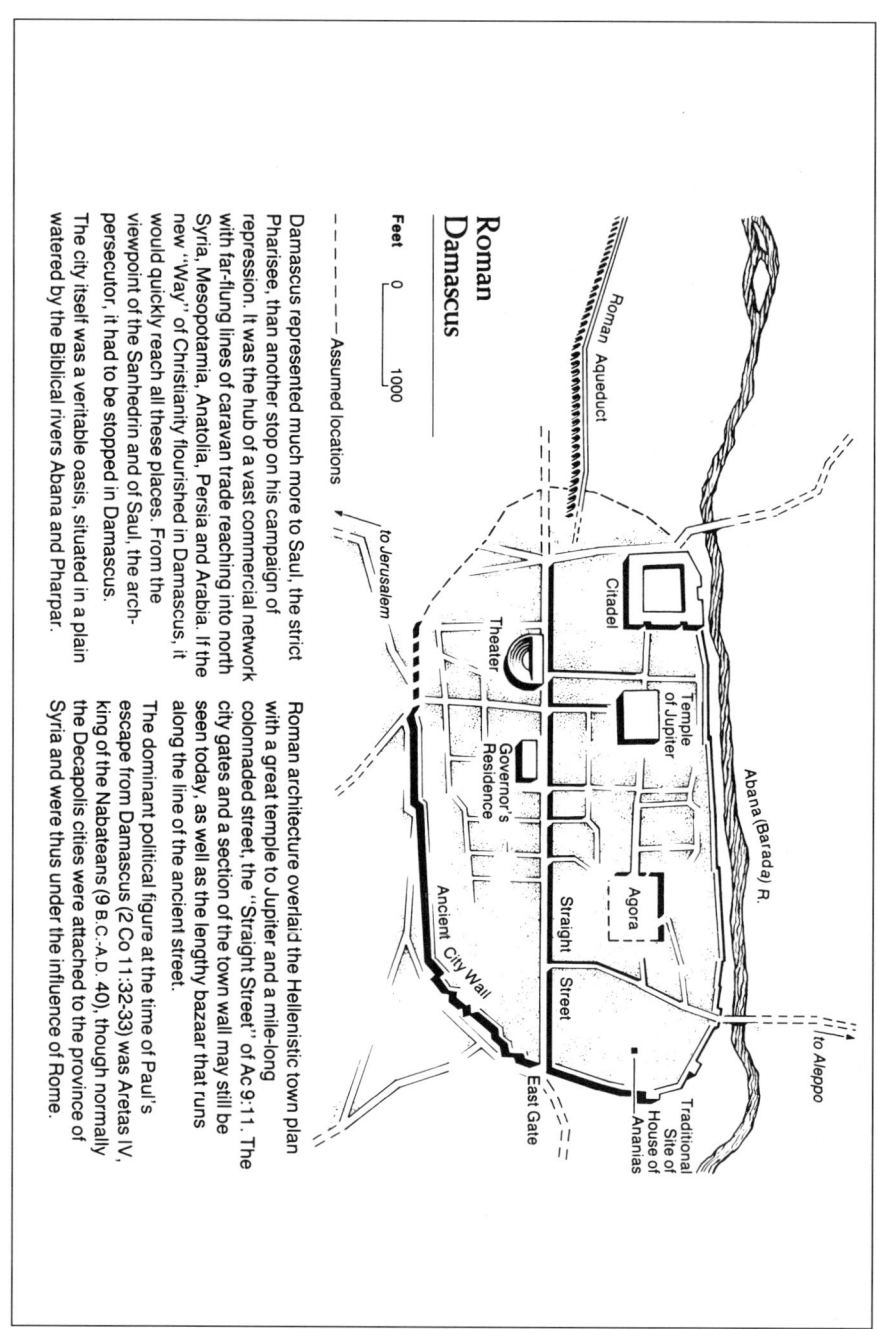

Roman Damascus

Feet 0 — 1000

- - - - - Assumed locations

Damascus represented much more to Saul, the strict Pharisee, than another stop on his campaign of repression. It was the hub of a vast commercial network with far-flung lines of caravan trade reaching into north Syria, Mesopotamia, Anatolia, Persia and Arabia. If the new "Way" of Christianity flourished in Damascus, it would quickly reach all these places. From the viewpoint of the Sanhedrin and of Saul, the arch-persecutor, it had to be stopped in Damascus.

The city itself was a veritable oasis, situated in a plain watered by the Biblical rivers Abana and Pharpar.

Roman architecture overlaid the Hellenistic town plan with a great temple to Jupiter and a mile-long colonnaded street, the "Straight Street" of Ac 9:11. The city gates and a section of the town wall may still be seen today, as well as the lengthy bazaar that runs along the line of the ancient street.

The dominant political figure at the time of Paul's escape from Damascus (2 Co 11:32-33) was Aretas IV, king of the Nabateans (9 B.C.-A.D. 40), though normally the Decapolis cities were attached to the province of Syria and were thus under the influence of Rome.

Taken from **NIV STUDY BIBLE**. Copyright © 1986 by The Zondervan Corporation. Used by permission of Zondervan Publishing House.

Session 5

Peter's Ministry

Acts 10–12

Approaching This Study

The ongoing and spectacular influence of the Holy Spirit continues to amaze us as we travel into the Book of Acts. Just as He promised, Jesus had not left His disciples comfortless. The Holy Spirit's power and presence is evident, intervening in different ways to steer His people in the right direction and ensure the church's growth. It is comforting for us today to witness the Holy Spirit's powerful influence on Peter. God and His angels intervened to give direction to Peter and, ultimately, the Christian church.

Even as God piloted His early church in the way of truth, so the Spirit continued to guide and direct His children. He does this today through His Word. Although there have been periods in history when the institutional church has strayed from the truth of God's Word, the Holy Spirit continued to work through that Word, raising courageous individuals who, guided by the Holy Spirit, redirected the church. We can remain confident that the Spirit still cares for the spiritual health of believers. He will always lead them through whatever challenges to the faith may arise.

An Overview

Unit Reading

The story of Peter and Cornelius in Acts 10 lends itself well to a dramatic reading. Someone should volunteer to take the part of Cornelius and, still another, the voice of Peter. One volunteer should read the words of the Lord. The rest of the group may read the words of the men sent by Cornelius to Peter. One final reader should voice the narrator's part. Whoever volunteered for the narrator may continue to read aloud Acts 11–12.

The Message in Brief

Peter's ongoing ministry that had recently brought about the healing of Aeneas and the resurrection of Tabitha continues into Caesarea. A Roman centurion by the name of Cornelius receives a vision from the Lord. An angel commands Cornelius to send men to Joppa to bring Peter to Cornelius's house in Caesarea. Meanwhile, Peter has a vision in which a variety of animals, at least some of which the Jews considered "unclean" (that is, unlawful to eat), descend on a sheet from heaven. The Lord commands Peter to eat the animals because everything God has made is now "clean." Once Peter arrives in Caesarea, he shares the Gospel of Jesus Christ with Cornelius and his household, whereupon the Spirit descends and the whole group is baptized. Peter realizes that in the vision God is telling him that the Gentiles are God's chosen. In the city of Antioch, many Gentiles become Christians. Barnabas is sent from Jerusalem to oversee their congregations. As persecution breaks out, James is martyred and Peter is imprisoned. An angel miraculously frees Peter from prison, and he returns to his fellow believers in the city. The Lord strikes dead Herod, the man responsible for the persecution.

Working with the Text

Peter Meets Cornelius (Acts 10)

1. Caesarea was the headquarters for the Roman armies in Palestine. Cornelius was a "centurion" in the Roman army. He commanded a military unit consisting of about 100 men. His military unit was part of a Roman regiment of about 600 men. This regiment was known as the "Italian" regiment. Ten of these regiments would compose a Roman "legion." How does the author of Acts describe Cornelius and his family? How are his prayers and gifts to the poor valued by God? Where was Peter when Cornelius sent his two servants and a soldier to bring him to Caesarea?

2. It was common for houses of Peter's day to have flat roofs with outside stairways. The flat roofs were often used as places for contemplation, prayer, and relaxation. Peter stayed with Simon the tanner. One day he climbed onto Simon's roof to pray. While praying, he experienced a

vision. Describe it. In Leviticus 11, God outlined for Israel which animals were "clean" and could be eaten, and which were "unclean" and should not be eaten. Read Leviticus 11:1–8 and list some of the "unclean" animals.

3. Caesarea was located about 30 miles north of Joppa. Peter and his companions traveled to Joppa in a little more than a day. When Peter arrived at Cornelius's house, what did Cornelius do and how did Peter respond? How did this reflect Peter's ongoing determination to give God full glory? Jewish law taught Jews not to associate with a Gentile. How had Peter's vision established a new paradigm for interacting with the Gentiles?

4. As Peter summarized the ministry of Jesus Christ to Cornelius and his household, he focused on several points.

a. With what was Jesus "anointed" at his Baptism? (The name "Messiah" is Hebrew for "the anointed one." The Greek word for the same is "Christ.")

b. Who were witnesses to Jesus' resurrection? How did Peter make it clear that Jesus' resurrection was not only spiritual, but also physical?

c. What is received by those who believe in Jesus?

5. There were some circumcised believers (Jewish Christians) who had traveled with Peter to Joppa. When they saw Cornelius and his household speaking in tongues and praising God, of what were they convinced? How many Jewish Christians had accompanied Peter and witnessed the outpouring of the Spirit on this Roman household (Acts 11:12)?

Moving from Jerusalem to Antioch (Acts 11)

1. Notice how the Jewish Christians in Jerusalem described the Gentiles who did not observe Jewish law as "uncircumcised men." What did the Jewish Christians accuse Peter of doing while he was in Caesarea ministering to the "uncircumcised men"?

2. As Peter defended intermingling with the Gentiles in Caesarea, he remembered how the Lord had promised to initiate a different kind of Baptism than that offered by John the Baptist. What was the difference between the two Baptisms (Acts 11:16; 19:4–6; Mark 1:4, 8)?

3. After the persecution had scattered believers from Jerusalem into the world, to whom did they first spread the message of Jesus Christ? Some began preaching to the Greek Gentiles, particularly in Antioch. Who was the first leader from Jerusalem sent to Antioch to oversee the new ministries there? Who did he seek for help? And what were believers first called in Antioch?

Peter's Escape and the End of Herod (Acts 12)

1. The Herod of this chapter was the grandson of the Herod who had attempted to kill the infant Jesus in Bethlehem (Matthew 2:1). He was also the nephew of the Herod who had tried Jesus (Luke 23:8–12). Certainly, Herod was weary of dealing with the ongoing influence of Jesus Christ! This Herod died in A.D. 44, so the events in this chapter must have happened shortly beforehand. Notice, then, that more than 10 years have passed since Christ's ascension and the miracle of Pentecost. What had Herod done to James, the brother of John, one of the sons of Zebedee? How was this a fulfillment of Jesus' prophecy (Matthew 20:20–23)?

2. When Peter was arrested, how many soldiers were assigned to guard him? These guards would have been grouped in fours and assigned different watches. What did Herod hope to do with Peter? How were the four guards arranged on the night of Peter's escape? Describe how the angel freed Peter.

3. After his escape, Peter went to the house of Mary, who was the mother of John Mark. John Mark was the author of the Gospel of Mark. Who answered the door when Peter knocked? How does her reaction seem very human and real? Peter asked those in the house to report his adventure to James. But hadn't James been beheaded? This was a different James. Which James was this (Galatians 1:19; Mark 6:3)?

4. What was Herod's reaction when he learned of Peter's escape? What happened to the guards? Herod was pleased because he was able to make peace with the citizens of two towns in Phoenicia (today we would call this area Lebanon). Why did the citizens make peace with Herod? In contrast to the apostles, did Herod give glory to God for his accomplishment? What happened to him as a result?

Applying the Message

1. It was difficult for the early Christians to believe that Jesus' promise of grace and salvation was to be given to the Gentiles as well as the Jews. The debate was settled with the obvious outpouring of the Holy Spirit on the Gentiles. Notice how heavily involved the Holy Spirit was in the formation and growth of the early church. How was the Spirit's involvement a fulfillment of Jesus' promise in John 16:12–15? What comfort can be found in knowing the Christian church has been guided throughout its history by the Holy Spirit?

2. Notice some of the parallels between Peter's imprisonment and escape and Jesus' death and resurrection. When did Herod arrest Peter (Acts 12:3–4)? When was Jesus arrested (Matthew 26:17)? What celestial figure was an integral part of Peter's escape (Acts 12:7–10)? And what celestial being rolled the stone away from Jesus' tomb (Matthew 28:2–3)? How did the guards react to the angel of the Lord at Jesus' resurrection (Matthew 28:4)? And how did the guards react to Peter's escape (Acts 12:18)? How were the guards silenced after Jesus' resurrection (Matthew 28:12–15)? How were they silenced after Peter's escape (Acts 12:19)? Many parallel accounts are found in Scripture. How does this suggest God's ongoing influence in directing the course of history? What does this suggest about His Lordship over time and space?

Taking the Message Home

Review

Read carefully Acts 10–12 once again and try to create a portrait of Peter's character. How would you describe him? Support your description by examples from these chapters.

Looking Ahead

Before the next session read Acts 13–14. Pay particular attention to the manner in which the Word of God spread and how resistance to the Gospel arose everywhere. Is the Gospel received differently today?

Working Ahead

Complete one or more of the following before the next session:

1. Ask your pastor to help you find the names of missionaries and their families working outside of the country. Then hold these servants of the Lord and their families in your prayers.

2. Christians are called upon to witness their faith, particularly to unbelievers. But what happens when those to whom we witness merely scoff and remain grounded in their faithlessness? Can anyone be forced to believe? What do you think the Christian's response should be toward those who continue to reject the Lord?

3. Look up the Greek gods Zeus and Hermes in an encyclopedia. Who were they and what roles did they allegedly perform? Be ready to report on these two gods at the beginning of the next session.

Did You Know That . . . ?

A Jewish soldier by the name of Josephus lived between A.D. 37 and A.D. 95. At the beginning of the war between the Romans and the Jews that culminated in the destruction of Jerusalem around A.D. 70, Josephus displayed tremendous valor and shrewdness. By the time the stronghold he defended was finally conquered, he had gained the admiration of the Roman general Vespasian. Josephus became a renowned historian of the Jews. One historical recollection revolves around Herod's last days (Acts 12:19b–23). Josephus claims that early on the second day of a festival in Caesarea, Herod wore a silver robe. The rising sun made his clothes shine so brightly that those who saw it proclaimed him a god. He neither acknowledged the claim nor denied it; but, soon after, he saw an owl sitting above his head and believed it was a messenger of evil in accordance with a prophecy once made to him. Suddenly he was seized with violent internal pains and carried home. He died five days later at the age of 54.

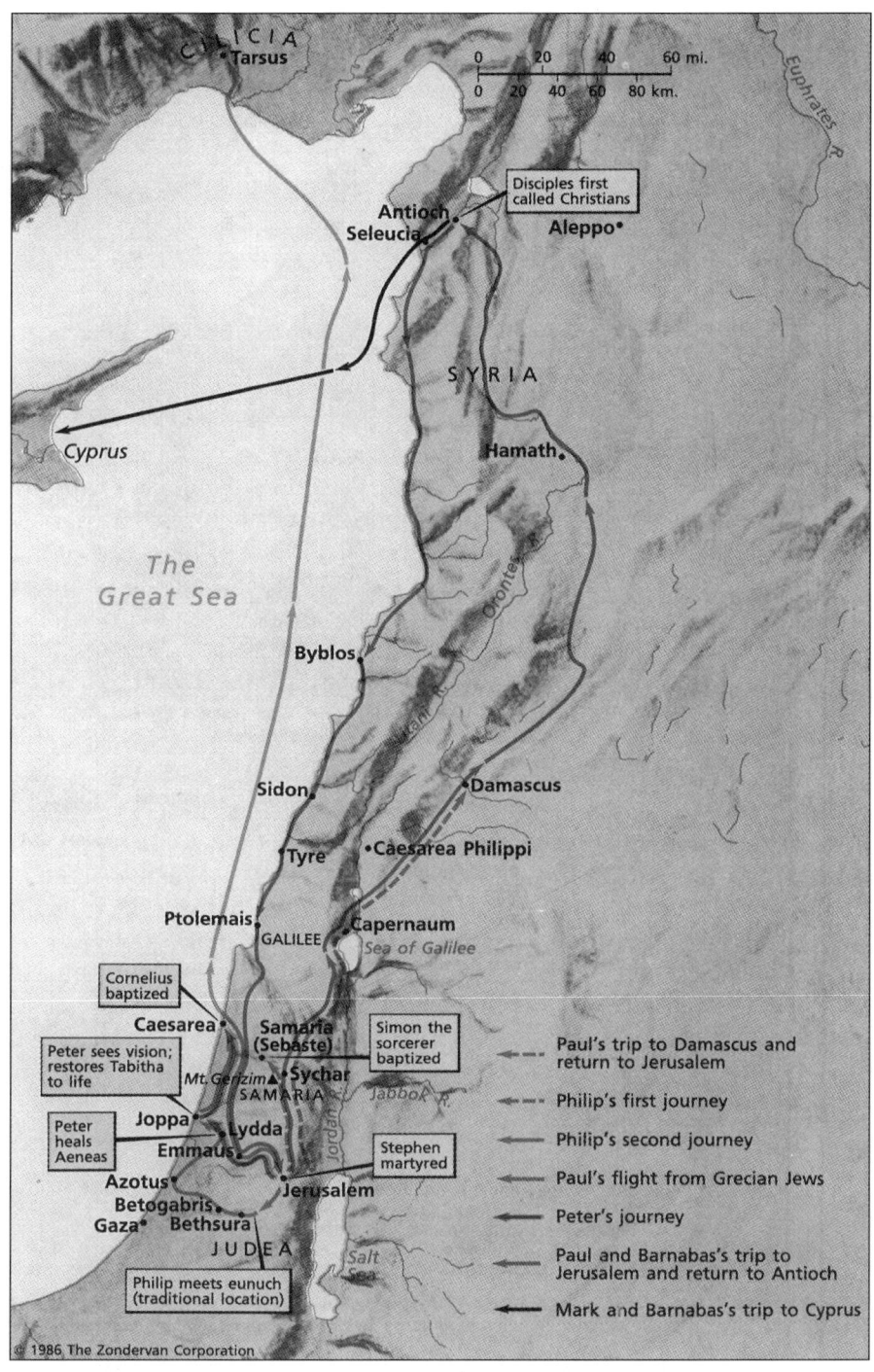

Taken from **NIV STUDY BIBLE**. Copyright © 1986 by The Zondervan Corporation.
Used by permission of Zondervan Publishing House.

Session 6

Paul's First Missionary Journey

Acts 13–14

Approaching This Study

As the story of the early church continues in Acts 13, the narration begins to shift away from Jerusalem into the various missionary journeys of Paul. The work of the Holy Spirit remains at the forefront of it all. Multitudes of people turn to the Lord Jesus and receive salvation. Inevitably, resistance arises against Paul's message, but he is never deterred. Filled with the Holy Spirit, Paul is empowered to preach the message of God's love in Christ. Throughout Paul's missionary journeys, the Spirit's guidance is evident. The Holy Spirit leads Paul to certain areas of the Roman Empire while directing him away from others. For this first missionary journey, the Holy Spirit calls Paul and Barnabas out of Antioch, across the island of Cyprus, and into the provinces of Asia Minor and Galatia. Paul always submits to God's will in these matters, recognizing that only the Lord knows which areas will be most responsive to the Gospel. On this first missionary journey we get a breathtaking glimpse of Paul's courage and determination that will continue to serve him throughout his ministry. The fanaticism that caused him to ruthlessly persecute the early Christian church now motivates him to sacrifice all he has, even his life if necessary, for the sake of the Lord Jesus. Christians in America are not usually called upon to be martyred for their faith, but all of us are called to testify to Jesus as He leads us by the ongoing power of His Spirit.

An Overview

Unit Reading

This session's reading involves the missionary journey of Paul and Barnabas through Cyprus and into the area we call Turkey today. As someone reads this section, track their journey on the map.

The Message in Brief

As the believers worship in Antioch, the Holy Spirit directs them to send Barnabas and Paul on a missionary journey to spread God's message of grace in Jesus Christ. On the island of Cyprus the two disciples encounter a sorcerer who has tremendous influence over the proconsul of that province. When Paul and Barnabas tell the proconsul about Jesus, the sorcerer attempts to refute their message. As a result, God strikes the sorcerer with blindness. In Pisidian Antioch (a different Antioch than that which is the center of Christian outreach), Paul boldly preaches to the Jews, explaining how the Old Testament points to Jesus. Some are converted, but many rise up in anger against his message. So Paul and Barnabas turn to the Gentiles and many believe. In Lystra, Paul and Barnabas are mistakenly thought to be Greek gods, and they must restrain the fanatical crowd from worshiping them as they attempt to spread Jesus' message. Irate Jews from several nearby cities enter Lystra and plot to murder Paul for his bold preaching. Afterwards, Paul and Barnabas return to Antioch and share their experiences with the other disciples.

Working with the Text

Paul's Sermon to the People of Pisidian Antioch (Acts 13)

1. List the five prophets and teachers residing in Antioch according to Acts 13:1. What relationship did Manaen have with Herod? Who called upon the disciples to set apart Paul and Barnabas for a missionary journey?

2. Where did Paul, Barnabas, and John first preach the Gospel in Salamis? Where did they begin preaching in Pisidian Antioch (Acts 13:14)? Where did they begin in Iconium (Acts 14:1)? Why do you think this was their common practice (Acts 13:45–46)?

3. Paul and Barnabas encountered a Jewish sorcerer in Paphos. His name was Bar-Jesus or Elymas. The proconsul (the Roman commander of the province), Sergius Paulus, was interested in hearing Paul's message; but Elymas hoped to keep him from believing the Gospel message. What was the consequence of Elymas's sin and how did it affect Sergius Paulus?

4. How would you describe Paul's strategy in preaching to the Jews of Pisidion Antioch? But was his message only for the Jews (v. 26)? Paul referred to several passages of Old Testament prophecy to prove Jesus was truly the Messiah. What does Psalm 2:7 quoted in Acts 13:33 prove about Jesus? What does Psalm 16:10 quoted in Acts 13:35–37 prove about Him? Was Paul's sermon "successful"? How?

5. How did many Jews feel about Paul according to verse 45? How did the Jews incite resistance against Paul and Barnabas (v. 50)? How did the two disciples respond as they left the city?

6. Unlike many of the Jews, the Gentiles were thrilled to hear the message of salvation through Jesus Christ. This was well and good, according to the author of Acts, because "all who were appointed to eternal life believed." Notice the word "appointed." How is this concept of God's appointment (often referred to as election) supported by Paul in Ephesians 2:8–9 and Ephesians 1:3–14?

The Lystra Misunderstanding (Acts 14:1–20)

1. To be sure, people who heard the Gospel for the first time must have thought the message peculiar. God became a human being and died for the sins of the world. But the Holy Spirit was determined to open people's hearts and minds to the truth of the message. With what did He accompany the disciples' preaching in order to persuade the hearers about God's truth (v. 3)? Did they convince everyone? Did resistance to their message stop them from preaching? What did they do instead?

2. Since Zeus was the patron god of Lystra, the city housed a temple dedicated to him. Furthermore, there existed an ancient legend that Zeus and Hermes had appeared in the flesh to the people of this area. Because one couple alone recognized the gods, the legend claimed, they were granted their wish to die together so that neither would have to mourn for the other. How might this legend help explain the citizens' reaction to Paul's miraculous healing of the lame man? Zeus was considered the chief Greek god, while Hermes was considered his messenger. How does this explain why the residents of Lystra mistook Paul for Hermes? What does this suggest about Barnabas's size and stature?

3. Paul nearly lost his life in Lystra. The Jews from Pisidian Antioch and Iconium stoned Paul and dragged him out of the city. They thought he was dead. But, after the disciples gathered around him, he got up *and went back into the city!* This was indeed a courageous act. But it was only one of many demonstrated by Paul. Turn to 2 Corinthians 11:23–28 and list the hardships endured by the apostle for the sake of the Gospel.

Returning to Antioch (Acts 14:21–28)

1. Paul not only brought the Good News to various cities throughout Asia Minor, he also helped establish local congregations there. On his way home to Antioch, how did he help ensure the congregations' survival (vv. 22–23)?

2. When Paul and Barnabas returned to Antioch, they shared their experiences with the other disciples. They described what "God had done through them" and "how He had opened the door of faith to the Gentiles." How do Paul and Barnabas glorify the Lord by their account?

Applying the Message

1. When Paul and Barnabas were expelled from Pisidian Antioch, they "shook the dust from their feet." Then they moved on. In what way might this be a good example for Christian evangelism?

2. When Paul spoke to the unbelieving Jews in Pisidian Antioch, he made it clear that since they had rejected the Gospel, he would turn to the Gentiles with the Gospel. In other words, when one group rejects Jesus, He simply goes to another. Can you see God working in the same way today? Give some examples.

3. After Paul preached the Gospel in Lystra, Jews from Antioch and Iconium tried to stone Paul to death. But Paul got right back on his feet and kept preaching. We have to admire his courage and persistence! In what ways do you think you have experienced rejection after witnessing to the Lord? Why should rejection not be a surprise?

Taking the Message Home

Review

As you review Acts 13–14, consider again Paul's message to the Jews in Pisidian Antioch. Notice how Paul approached the Gospel of Jesus Christ through the stories and promises of the Old Testament. What does this suggest about the importance of the Old Testament for contemporary Christians?

Looking Ahead

In the next session we will study Acts 15–16. After reading this section, write down those events that seem most remarkable or most confusing. Be ready to share your comments with others in the group.

Working Ahead

Complete one or more of the following before the next session:

1. Discover who is on your congregation's "council" or "board of directors." Introduce yourself to one or more of them and ask them what they enjoy most about their work as a congregational leader.

2. Sometimes the Lord has directed His people through dreams or visions, or through the words of an angel. When individuals feel they have experienced something so dramatic, they may reasonably question whether their direction is from God, from the devil, or simply a hallucination. Read 2 Timothy 3:16–17. How do these verses suggest one can discern whether the direction or instruction is God-pleasing or not?

3. Fortune-telling is a popular pastime, but when people take it seriously they disobey God's will (Leviticus 19:26). Why do you think the Lord views fortune-telling as a sin?

Did You Know That . . . ?

Scholars have contemplated how and why Saul's name was changed to Paul. There certainly are biblical precedents for a name change after an individual has been touched in a special way by the Lord. Abram's name, for example, was changed to Abraham once he received God's promise of being the father of many nations. And that makes sense. The name "Abram" meant "exalted father," whereas "Abraham" meant "the father of many." Jacob's name was changed to Israel after he wrestled with God. And that's appropriate, too, because the name Israel means "he struggles with God." Simon's name was changed to Peter after the Lord acknowledged that his kind of rock-like faith would be instrumental in building God's church. The name Peter, after all, means "rock." But what about Saul changing his name to Paul? The name "Paul" simply means "little." Many Jews in Paul's day had a given name in Hebrew and a later name in Greek. Perhaps this was the Greek name given to Paul as a child. Or perhaps it was the name he assumed because he had been so successful in preaching to the proconsul Sergius Paulus (Acts 13:6–7). In any case, the new name recorded in Scripture was an indication of his new life through faith in Jesus. From here on out, Saul will be known as Paul.

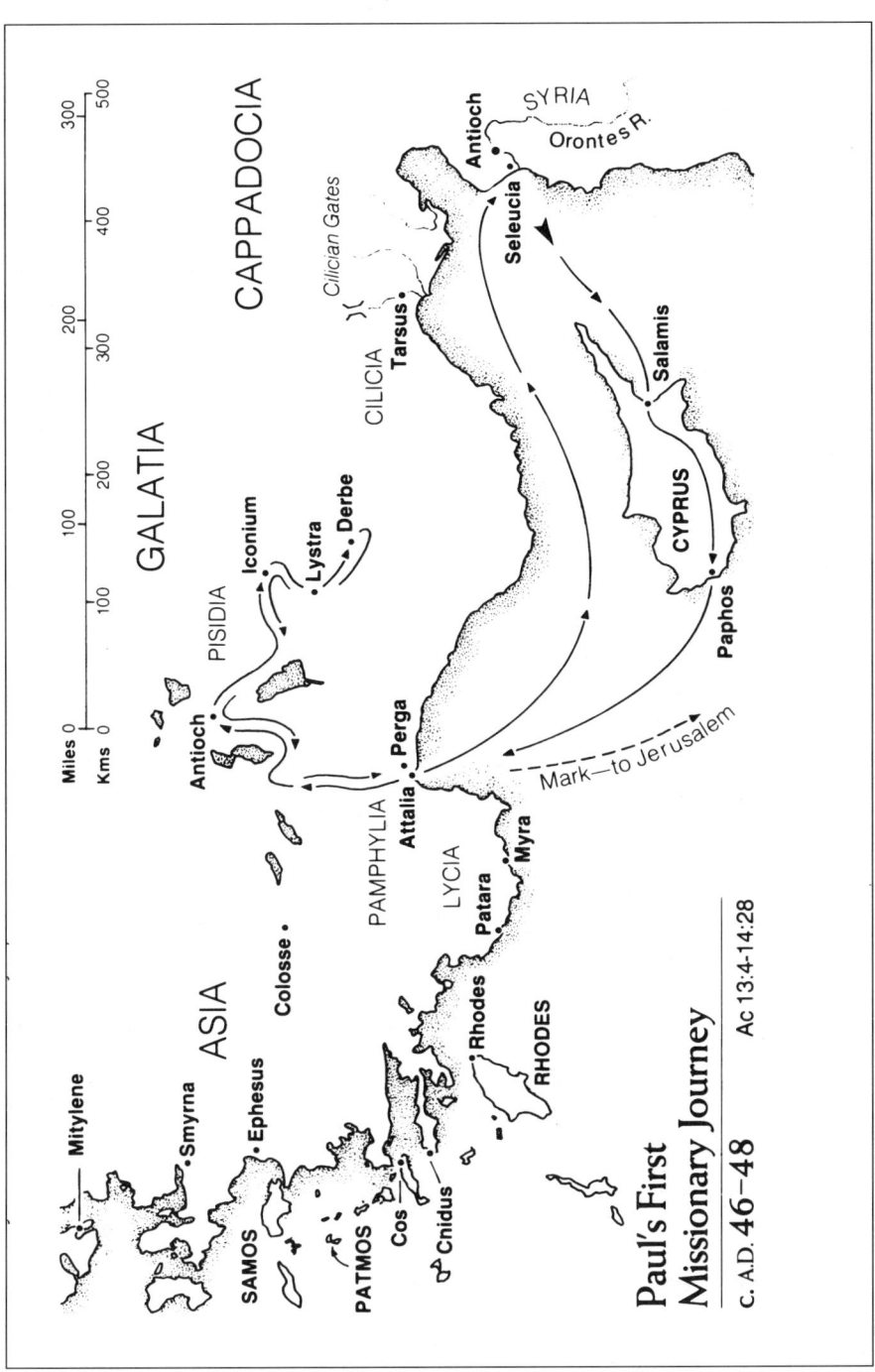

Session 7

The Jerusalem Council and Paul's Second Missionary Journey

Acts 15–16

Approaching This Study

The division between Jewish Christians and Gentile Christians reached its climax when Jewish Christians from Judea began visiting the largely Gentile church in Antioch demanding the Gentiles be circumcised. Paul and Barnabas, who had watched the Spirit descend on many Gentiles, were outraged by these demands. These requirements struck at the very heart of the Gospel that proclaims people are saved purely by the grace of God in Jesus Christ and not by any rites or works they can accomplish themselves. It was the first major attempt by well-meaning but sinful believers to add "clauses" or an "addendum" to the free gift of salvation won by Jesus Christ. It continues to stand as a warning for churches today.

The Jerusalem council, led by the Holy Spirit, reached a conclusion that satisfied the Gentile Christians and allowed the proclamation of the Gospel to proceed unhindered. Paul began his second missionary journey, revisiting many believers with whom he had become acquainted during his first missionary journey, while sharing the Gospel with Gentiles who by the Spirit's power came to faith. At every step, the Holy Spirit guided, empowered, and protected Paul just as He continues to guide and protect believers today.

An Overview

Unit Reading

Ask a volunteer to read Acts 15–16. The rest of the group should list on a sheet of newsprint the names of the people mentioned in this section. How many of these names are familiar to you? Why are they familiar? Which ones are unfamiliar?

The Message in Brief

After Paul's first missionary journey, Paul and Barnabas remain in Antioch for more than a year. In time, however, they are called to Jerusalem to help wrestle with questions surrounding the tide of Gentiles joining the Christian church. Should the Gentiles be required to follow the ceremonial laws of the Old Testament as do the Jewish Christians? Or should they be held to a different standard of behavior? Since Paul and Barnabas have had much experience working with Gentiles, their input is important. The church leaders in Jerusalem, persuaded by Paul, who was guided by the Holy Spirit working through God's Word, decide the Gentiles should not be burdened with most of the Old Testament regulations. The Gentile Christians are encouraged to follow a couple of regulations that would be most offensive to the Jewish Christians, if ignored.

Paul decides to retrace his journey and visit the Christian congregations established on his first missionary route. Along the way, he meets Timothy, who will become one of his best friends and supporters. He baptizes Lydia, the first recorded convert in Europe. Paul is imprisoned for his preaching, but after a violent earthquake frees him from prison, he baptizes a terrified jailer and his family.

Working with the Text

The First Church Council (Acts 15:1–35)

1. Notice how Luke writes that men came "down" to Antioch from Judea (15:1) and that Paul and Barnabas went "up" to Jerusalem (15:2). Although Antioch was north of Jerusalem and Judea, the words refer to elevation rather than direction. Jerusalem and Judea were higher than the city of Antioch, which rested by the sea. As Paul and Barnabas traveled south to Jerusalem, what did they share with their Christian brethren along the way?

2. Some of the Jewish Christians from Judea came to the church in

Antioch, a mostly Gentile congregation, and demanded the Gentiles be circumcised or they could not be saved. Look up "circumcision" in a Bible dictionary. What was the purpose of this rite in the Old Testament? Look now at Colossians 2:11–12. What has replaced circumcision since the coming of Christ?

3. Notice how some Christians still viewed themselves as Pharisees (v. 5). At this time Christianity was not a separate entity from Judaism. What did these Jewish Christians demand of the Gentiles? Who was the first to stand and defend the Gentiles? Did he suggest there should be a distinction between Jew and Gentile? Why or why not?

4. What finally convinced the other disciples in Jerusalem that the Gentiles were also saved by the grace of God in Jesus Christ and should not be required to follow Old Testament ceremonial regulations? How did James, the brother of Jesus, support this decision? What few requirements did they ask the Gentiles to follow? Which of these suggestions do you think are always appropriate for Christians to follow, and which do you think were requested of the Gentiles simply to keep them from offending Jewish believers?

5. Acts 15:13–21 suggests James, the brother of Jesus, made the final judgment about the Gentiles. What does this suggest about his "clout" among the believers in Jerusalem? Who accompanied Paul and Barnabas back to Antioch with the decision rendered by the Jerusalem council? What gifts did they possess (v. 32)?

The Beginning of Paul's Second Missionary Journey (Acts 15:36–16:40)

1. What plan did Paul and Barnabas devise to strengthen the churches established on their first missionary journey? Barnabas wanted to bring John Mark, the author of the Gospel of Mark, with them. What did Paul think about this idea? Why? See Acts 15:38 and Acts 13:13. Even though John Mark had disappointed Paul and Barnabas, Barnabas wanted to "forgive and forget." In what way was Barnabas's desire consistent with the attitude he displayed toward Paul in Acts 9:26–27?

2. In Lystra, Paul met Timothy. Of what ethnic origin was his mother? Of what ethnic origin was his father? Even though the Jerusalem council had determined Gentiles need not be circumcised, Paul had Timothy circumcised anyway! Is this hypocrisy? Why do you think Paul insisted on this (1 Corinthians 9:19–23)?

3. Isn't it interesting how Paul was restrained from traveling to certain areas, while he was invited into other areas? Who directed his travels? What, in particular, convinced Paul to go to Macedonia? Notice Acts 16:10. Who now accompanied Paul?

4. When Paul and Silas reached the city of Philippi in Macedonia, to whom did they speak at the river? Where was Lydia from and why do you imagine she was in Philippi? Purple cloth was very expensive in Paul's day. What does this suggest about Lydia's affluence? She wor-

shiped God but had not yet heard about the resurrection of Jesus Christ. What did she and her household do immediately upon the Holy Spirit's conversion?

5. While in Philippi, Paul and Barnabas encountered a fortune-teller. Interestingly, she followed along and called God the "Most High God." Turn to Mark 5:7. What did the man possessed by an evil spirit call Jesus? After many days of her hollering, Paul finally turned around and exorcized her. How did her owners react to this? Why?

6. How did Paul and Silas "evangelize" even while in prison? Both disciples were released miraculously from prison. How did this release happen? What was the jailer's reaction to their release? After the Philippian jailer became a Christian, how did his life change (v. 34)?

7. Roman citizens were protected by law from public beatings and beatings without trials. When the city officials learned they had violated Paul and Silas' rights, how did these officials hope to appease the two disciples?

Applying the Message

1. One of the interesting dimensions of Lydia's conversion and the jailer's conversion revolves around their households. Not only were these

two individuals baptized, but their whole households were baptized as well. Surely, the Philippian jailer was the head of his household; and, because Lydia's husband is never mentioned, it seems probable that she, too, headed her household. So it's no wonder they would have had the authority to make certain everyone in their families was baptized. Even in households where a believer is not the head, how can that believer influence others in his or her family?

2. The Jerusalem council decided Gentile Christians should not eat food offered to idols. The pagans of Paul's time would offer meat to their false gods, reserving part of the food for dinner or for sale at the market. Christians would sometimes eat this food just because it was food. Paul, in 1 Corinthians 8, makes clear there is nothing intrinsically sinful about the food; but, if those who are weaker in the faith would be offended by their fellow Christians eating such meat, they should be considerate of their feelings and not consume the meat. Can you think of any contemporary parallels that would call for a Christian abstaining from a certain practice, not because it is wrong but because it might offend other Christians who are weaker in their faith?

3. Even in our day, how do you think man-made rules might infringe on the grace of God? In other words, how do some churches add requirements for their members' assurance of salvation?

Taking the Message Home

Review

After reviewing these two chapters of Acts, write a summary of the story surrounding the jailer in Philippi. Find the letter in the New Testament that was written to the church in Philippi and read Philippians 1:1–11. How does Paul feel about this church?

Looking Ahead

Scan Acts 17–19. In your Bible, find the New Testament letters written to three of the churches mentioned in this section. Add up the number of letters written to them.

Working Ahead

Complete one or more of the following before the next session:

1. Look at the map of Paul's second missionary journey found in this book. Locate Thessalonica, Berea, Athens, Corinth, and Ephesus. Which city is located in the area known as Turkey today? Which cities are in Greece?

2. Focus on the preacher named Apollos. Write what you can learn about him from Acts 18:24–28, and be ready to share your impressions with the group.

3. In an encyclopedia, look up the goddess Artemis. Who was she and what was her function? Turn to the map of Ephesus in the next session and locate the temple of Artemis.

Did You Know That . . . ?

The site where Philippi rested is now deserted, but archaeologists have uncovered many sections of the city. For example, the marketplace where Paul and Silas were dragged and condemned to flogging and imprisonment (Acts 16:19) remains. Archaeologists have also uncovered a great arched gateway at the northwest edge of the city. This is probably the gate through which Paul and Silas exited in order to find a place by the river to pray (Acts 16:13). And about one mile west of the city runs the only river in the vicinity. This, no doubt, was the place the Gospel of Jesus Christ was first proclaimed in Europe—to the women who had gathered there, particularly to Lydia.

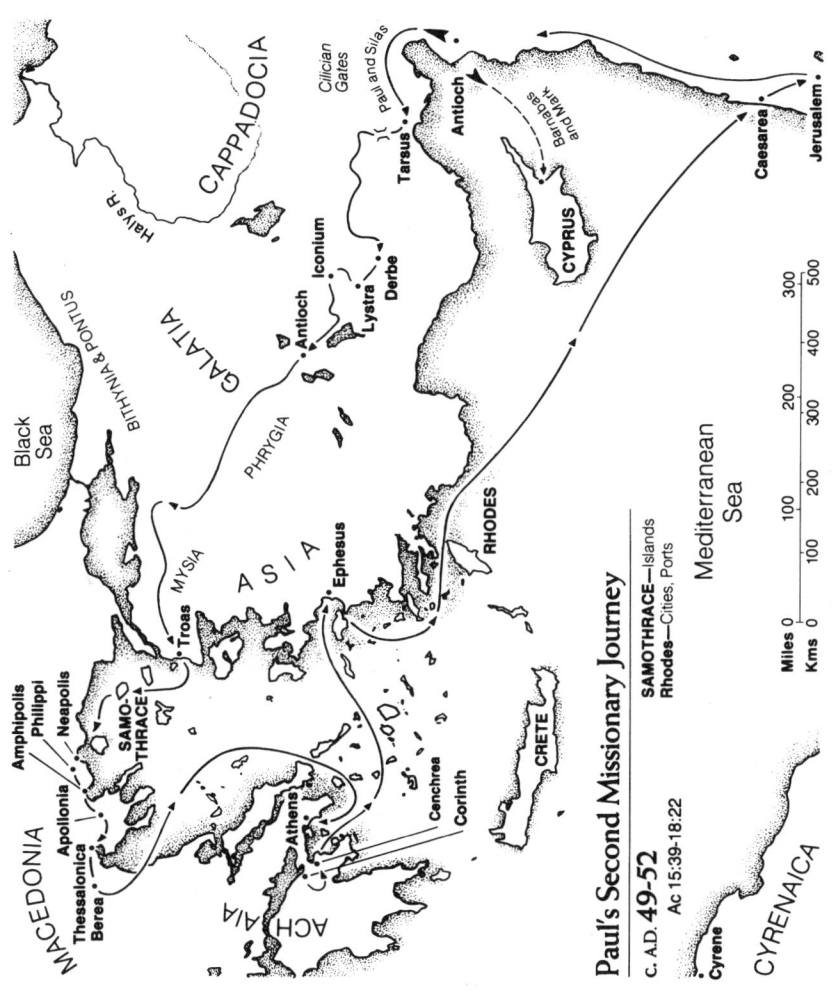

Taken from **NIV STUDY BIBLE**. Copyright © 1986 by The Zondervan Corporation. Used by permission of Zondervan Publishing House.

Session 8

On the Road Again

Acts 17–19

Approaching This Study

Everywhere Paul preached, it seemed, riots followed. His message threatened a number of people, particularly those Jews who could not grasp the concept of God's grace in Jesus Christ. They argued with him. How could salvation be a free gift from God? How could God die on the cross for people's sins? In their opinion, Paul taught heresy for which he should be put to death. But with confidence and courage, Paul continued to proclaim the Gospel from one city to the next. Some cities received his message wholeheartedly, while others only listened, amused and apathetic. Still others felt their livelihoods threatened by his message. Before reading Acts 17–19, read Jesus' parable of the sower in Matthew 13:3–9, 18–23. In this parable, Jesus accurately predicted the various ways in which people would respond to the Word of God. As you read the next few chapters in Acts, keep His words in mind and try to associate the various seeds with the responses of the Thessalonians, Bereans, Athenians, Corinthians, and Ephesians.

An Overview

Unit Reading

The Scripture reading for this section may be broken into locations. One volunteer should read about Paul's visit to Thessalonica (Acts 17:1–9), another about Berea (Acts 17:10–15), still another, Athens (Acts 17:16–34), and yet another, Corinth (Acts 18:1–17). The leader should finish reading about Paul's visit to Ephesus in Acts 18:18–19:41.

The Message in Brief

Paul continues on his second missionary journey. Having been released from the Philippian prison, he reaches Thessalonica; and, although through his message the Holy Spirit works to transform some hearts, many of the Jews incite a riot within the city. So, under cover of night, Paul and Silas escape and arrive at Berea. They receive a noble response to their preaching. Several Jews from Thessalonica begin to stir up trouble in Berea, so Paul journeys on to Athens. There he confronts a secularized and sophisticated crowd who display interest in Paul's ideas but are not particularly moved to follow Jesus. From Athens Paul journeys to Corinth, where he befriends two outstanding believers named Aquila and Priscilla.

After returning to Antioch, Paul begins his third missionary journey. He reaches the city of Ephesus, where he discovers a number of people who are followers of John the Baptist but have not yet heard about Jesus. After baptizing them in the name of Jesus, Paul begins preaching in the synagogue and performing many miracles. Ephesus has a temple devoted to the goddess Artemis. Many of the townspeople earn their living creating artifacts for this cult worship and are outraged by Paul's preaching. As a result, a riot against Paul breaks out.

Working with the Text

The Second Missionary Journey Continues (Acts 17:1–18:22)

1. In Paul's day, the city of Thessalonica had more than 200,000 people. A sizeable number of Jews lived in the city, enough to establish and maintain their own synagogue. Because he was a rabbi, that is, a Jewish teacher, Paul was invited to teach in the synagogue. He used the opportunity to exalt Jesus as the long-awaited Messiah. How would you describe the results of his preaching?

2. How did the "jealous" Jews respond to Paul and Silas in Thessalonica? For what did the jealous Jews attempt to charge Jason and other Christians before the city officials? How was their charge only partially true?

3. After reading about Paul's work in Berea, compare the response of the Bereans to that of the Thessalonians. Would you describe Paul's work as "successful" in Berea? Why or why not?

4. When Paul arrived in Athens, he began debating with the Epicureans and the Stoics. The Stoics believed people should live in harmony with nature while focusing on independence and self-sufficiency. The Epicureans felt the highest good was happiness, although they understood happiness as more than instant gratification. How did the author, Luke, indicate that most of the Athenians were all talk and no action (Acts 17:21)?

5. Paul stood up at the Areopagus (the "hill of Ares") and attempted to persuade the Athenians about the importance of knowing Jesus Christ. Describe his strategy in addressing the crowds. How did he flatter them into listening to him and use part of their pagan religion to point to Jesus Christ? Do you think this was a clever strategy? Would you consider the results "successful"?

6. Where had Priscilla and Aquila recently come from before they settled in Corinth? Why had they moved? Once again, where did Paul begin his ministry in Corinth? When he was rejected, to whom did he turn? From an inscription found in the city of Delphi, it is known that Gallio was proconsul of Achaia in A.D. 51–52. He was the brother of the philosopher Seneca, who also tutored Nero. What was Gallio's response to the charges against Paul?

7. Sometimes in Paul's day, people would take vows to express thanks for their deliverance from very dangerous situations. How might that explain the reason for Aquila (or Paul—it is not clear who is mentioned here) shaving his head before leaving Corinth (Acts 18:18)?

The Third Missionary Journey Begins: Ephesus (Acts 18:23–19:41)

1. How would you describe Apollos and his preaching? Now read 2 Corinthians 10:10–11 and 2 Peter 3:15–16. Describe Paul's preaching. After Apollos had been further instructed in the Christian faith by Priscilla and Aquila, he became Paul's successor in Corinth. He became the pastor of the Corinthian church. What difficulties arose as a result of this succession according to 1 Corinthians 3:1–9?

2. When Paul arrived in Ephesus, he encountered a group that followed the teachings of John the Baptist. They had not heard about the Holy Spirit nor about Baptism in the name of Jesus Christ. How did they react when the Holy Spirit descended upon them?

3. Typical of Paul's evangelistic style, he began preaching about Jesus in the synagogue of Corinth. After three months, resistance arose against his teaching and he was banned from the synagogue. Where did he go to discuss religion and how long did he remain there? Describe the pow-

erful way in which the Spirit manifested Himself through Paul during these days.

4. Ephesus was the home of a Jewish magician named Sceva (pronounced SEE-vah) and his seven sons. They attempted to cast out demons in the name of Jesus. Since they invoked the name of the Lord as a part of their act, how did the demons react to their attempts at exorcism? Ephesus was also a center of magical incantations. How did the sorcerers respond to the name of Jesus?

5. From Ephesus, Paul decided to travel through Macedonia and Achaia, then return to Jerusalem. Where did he hope to go after that (Acts 19:21)? He would finally reach his destination, but not in the way he anticipated! However, before Paul left, a disturbance arose in Ephesus. Who was behind it, and why was there so much concern about the Gospel's effect on the Ephesians? Describe what happened when the mob dragged Paul's companions, Gaius and Aristarchus, into the theater.

6. The city clerk of Ephesus was the most important local official available. He acted as an intermediary between Ephesus and the Roman government. How did he quiet the mob? How might the image of Artemis have "fallen from heaven" (Acts 19:35)?

Applying the Message

1. The Bereans were remarkable followers of Christ. Their notoriety arose from a determination to validate Paul's teachings through their own personal Scripture reading. Why is it important that Christian lay people follow their example? If more people read and studied the Bible, do you think there might exist fewer religious cults? Why?

2. One has to give Paul credit for his creative approach to preaching the Gospel in Athens. He found an altar whose inscription read "To an unknown god," and he explained how this unknown God could be known through Jesus Christ! Even though his approach was ingenious, the number of converts gained in Athens was not impressive. Humans can be extraordinarily creative and enthusiastic about preaching the Gospel, but that does not guarantee "success" in terms of numbers. Why do you think that is the case? See 1 Corinthians 12:3.

3. The temple of Artemis in Ephesus was one of the seven wonders of the world. People came from everywhere to see it. They would purchase silver shrines and images, providing Demetrius and the silversmiths of Ephesus a fabulous income. It's no wonder the silversmiths felt threatened by the Gospel of Jesus Christ! Can you think of contemporary examples where the message of Christianity might threaten economic interests?

Taking the Message Home

Review

Look over Acts 17–19. Although Paul wrote letters to the churches in Thessalonica, Corinth, and Ephesus, we have no record of his writing to the church in Athens. In what ways do you think the response of the Athenians to the Gospel is similar to that of people today?

Looking Ahead

Before the next session, read Acts 20–22. Paul completes his third missionary journey and is arrested in Jerusalem for inciting a riot. Isn't it remarkable how the simple message of the Gospel has the power to stir emotions? By the same token, the Gospel has the power to transform lives and inspire wondrous action. Some might call the message of Jesus' death and resurrection "absurd," or "fanciful," or "outrageous." But no one who really hears it can remain indifferent!

Working Ahead

Complete one or more of the following before the next session:

1. Paul's sermons may not have been terribly dynamic. After all, not all speeches are exciting. Some can be quite boring. Recall the most boring speech you ever heard and share your experience with others in the group. Do you remember anything that was said? In your opinion, what made the speech particularly tedious?

2. As a young man, Paul was taught by the most honored rabbi of the first century. His name was Gamaliel. Who was your favorite teacher? Was it a parent or an educator? Why was she or he so important in your life? In what way has your life been molded by his or her influence?

3. Paul was not only a Jew, he was also a Roman citizen. His Roman citizenship allowed him certain benefits and was eventually used by the Lord to bring Paul to Rome. What benefits do we receive from our citizenship? In what ways do you think our citizenship might be helpful for those who, like Paul, travel around the world?

Did You Know That . . . ?

Aquila (whose name means "eagle") and Priscilla (whose name means "ancient") were Jews from Asia Minor who migrated to Rome. They were exiled from Rome in A.D. 49 by the Emperor Claudius, who had all Jews expelled from the city. Nearly one year later they met Paul in Corinth. Aquila and Priscilla had much in common with Paul because all three were tentmakers. Paul lived with them in Corinth and they became partners in Christian evangelism. They even sailed with Paul to Ephesus during his second missionary journey, and they awaited his return from Antioch on the third missionary journey. During this time, they became acquainted with Apollos and instructed him in the faith. Following the death of Emperor Claudius, the edict of banishment was no longer in force and Aquila and Priscilla were able to return to Rome. Of the six times Aquila and Priscilla are mentioned in Scripture, Priscilla's name is put first in four references, suggesting she may have been a more prominent member of the church than he!

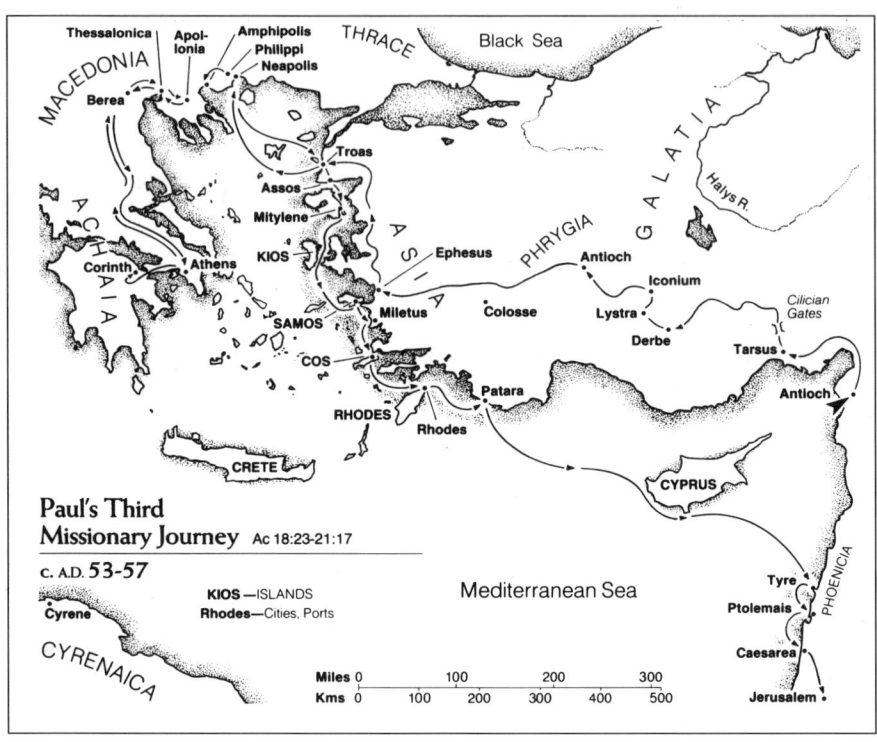

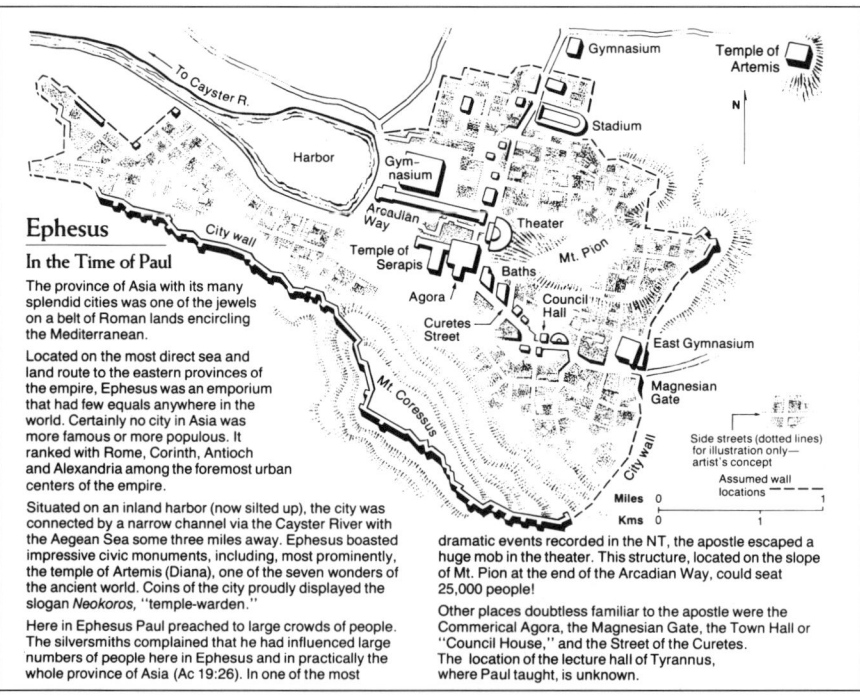

Session 9

The Third Missionary Journey Comes to a Difficult End

Acts 20–22

Approaching This Study

We've already witnessed a number of riots that erupted in various cities when Paul preached the Good News of grace and forgiveness in Jesus Christ. It was only a matter of time before the Roman Empire took notice of these disruptions. In Jerusalem, Christianity began to catch the eye of the empire. Palestine had always been a difficult area to govern; and when a riot ensued in Jerusalem, the largest and most important city in Palestine, it was only to be expected that Rome should be interested. Once again we witness hostile Jews following Paul from the province of Asia. This time they entered the capital city of Jewish belief—Jerusalem—enraged that Paul should attempt to bring his "heresy" there. Following the principle that "a good defense is a good offense," the Jews began to spread malicious gossip about Paul throughout the city, which, of course, culminated in confusion and disruption. Only because of a Roman commander's intervention was Paul saved from death. But once Paul fell into the hands of Rome, a long legal process began to build. Paul was patient as the process ran its course. He trusted completely in the governance and providence of the Lord. As the Roman government became more entwined in his case, he would grow closer to his intended destination: Rome itself.

An Overview

Unit Reading

Read aloud Acts 20–22 using two volunteers. One volunteer should be the voice of Paul, and another volunteer may read the rest of this section.

The Message in Brief

Paul's third missionary journey continues through Macedonia and Greece. In the city of Troas, he meets all night with the local Christians, preaching to them until midnight. One young man drifts asleep in an upstairs window, falls to the ground, and dies. God empowers Paul to raise him from the dead. As Paul's journey circles back to Jerusalem, he passes Ephesus and admonishes the Ephesian elders to remain faithful to Jesus' teachings. An ominous feeling builds concerning Paul's upcoming fate in Jerusalem, exacerbated by the prophet Agabus, who warns that Paul will be arrested and bound when he arrives in the city. Paul arrives in Jerusalem and begins preaching. Some of the hostile Jews from the province of Asia stir up hostility toward Paul by spreading false rumors. A riot ensues (again!), but Paul is saved from certain death by a Roman commander. Paul is arrested and pleads his case before the mob. The crowd continues to call for punishment, but when the Roman commander is about to flog Paul, he learns Paul is a Roman citizen. Since a Roman citizen cannot be handled so roughly, the Roman commander arranges for a trial before the Jewish Sanhedrin.

Working with the Text

The Third Missionary Journey Continues (Acts 20)

1. After the uproar in Ephesus, Paul continued his journey. He was accompanied by, among others, Aristarchus, Gaius, Timothy, Tychicus, and Trophimus. They all planned to rendezvous at Troas. What do the following passages tell us about these individuals:

a. Aristarchus (Acts 27:1–2; Acts 19:29; Colossians 4:10):

b. Timothy (Philippians 2:19–23; Acts 16:1; 2 Timothy 1:5):

c. Tychicus (Ephesians 6:21–22; Colossians 4:7–9):

d. Trophimus (Acts 21:29; 2 Timothy 4:20):

2. On what day of the week were the early Christians worshiping in Troas according to Acts 20:7? Until what time did Paul preach? And what happened to the young man, Eutychus, as he listened to Paul's sermon? How did Paul handle the situation?

3. Notice how the narrative in Acts 20:13 begins using the word "we." Luke, the author, was once again involved in Paul's ministry. They sailed to a number of cities but bypassed Ephesus (Acts 20:16). Can you think of any reason why Paul would want to avoid the city of Ephesus?

4. In Miletus, Paul sent for the elders of the Ephesian church. When Paul reviewed his work with them, what did he say was most important for them to understand (Acts 20:21)? Paul would travel to Jerusalem. What did he fear would happen there (v. 23)? About what future danger did Paul warn these church leaders (vv. 29–31)? What grieved the Ephesian elders most about Paul's farewell address to them (vv. 25, 38)?

Paul's Arrest in Jerusalem (Acts 21)

1. Paul continued his journey to Jerusalem by boat. The ship sailed southward to Tyre where the cargo was unloaded. This gave Paul time to visit with the local Christians. Fearful of what might happen to Paul, what did Luke and the other Christians do in Tyre?

2. A prophet named Agabus greeted Paul in Caesarea. How did Agabus, through an object lesson, demonstrate Paul's fate in Jerusalem? Why did this not deter Paul?

3. Sometimes Jews would separate or consecrate themselves for a period of time and offer total devotion to God. This was accomplished through the "Nazirite vow." Look up Numbers 6:2–12. List the practices that accompanied the vow. When and why would a Nazirite be forced to shave his head? What else would be required should his vow be defiled? The four Jewish Christians in Jerusalem, although they believed in the grace and forgiveness of God through Jesus Christ, wished to follow the custom of taking the Nazirite vow (Acts 21:23). Now many in Jerusalem had heard the rumor that Paul was forcing Jewish Christians to abstain from all Jewish practices. This was false, of course. How did Paul demonstrate the error of this rumor?

4. Paul had suffered before at the hands of some Jews who lived in the province of Asia. Now these same Jews arrived in Jerusalem. What false accusation about Paul did they proclaim all over the city? How did the citizens react? Who delivered Paul from certain death and where was he taken? Who did the Roman commander think Paul might be?

Paul's Defense (Acts 22)

1. Near the beginning of Acts, we read that Paul was instrumental in the martyrdom of Stephen. Was he the only Christian for whose death Paul was responsible? What does Paul himself say in Acts 22:4?

2. Paul recounts the miraculous vision of Jesus that was revealed on his way to Damascus. What details in this account seem new to you?

3. In Acts 22:17 we learn Paul's Damascus experience was not the only time he saw and heard the Lord. What happened to Paul after he had received his sight and was again in the Jerusalem temple? How did the Lord's words point to the beginning of the fulfillment of Isaiah 65:1 and Hosea 2:23?

4. There were three ways to gain Roman citizenship. One could receive it as a reward for outstanding service to the Roman Empire, one could purchase it at a hefty price, or one could be born into a family of Roman citizens. Somehow, Paul's father or grandfather must have gained such citizenship, because Paul was a citizen by birth. Roman citizens were excluded from degrading forms of punishment like crucifixion or being beaten with rods. It mystified the Roman commander why the Jews in Jerusalem were so upset with Paul. So what did the commander arrange as a way of discovering Paul's alleged crimes?

Applying the Message

1. Before returning to Jerusalem, Paul warned the elders of Ephesus about people who would distort the truth of the Gospel for their own gain. We witness the truth of his warning all the time. Many cults and false religions have arisen since the time of Paul. Why do you think it seems so easy to create a new cult or religion in America? What do you think would help prevent people from following such cults?

2. The Jews from Asia who followed Paul into Jerusalem spread vicious and untruthful rumors about him. The consequence of their lies was disastrous. How might Paul's painful experience motivate us to abstain from spreading gossip? The next time you hear something that discredits another's reputation, what will you do?

3. By this time, we begin to marvel at the extent of Paul's journeys, particularly under what we would consider primitive conditions. Many of us would like to imitate Paul, spreading the Gospel throughout the world, but we are physically and materially unable to accomplish this goal. Nevertheless, in what ways can we be instrumental in spreading Jesus' Word? How can we play an important role in fulfilling Jesus' Great Commission: "Go and make disciples of all nations, baptizing them in the name of the Father, Son and Holy Spirit, and teaching them to observe everything I have commanded you" (Matthew 28:19–20)?

Taking the Message Home

Review

Reread Acts 20–22. What attributes of Paul's personality impressed you the most in this section of Scripture? Why?

Looking Ahead

Read Acts 23–24 before the next session. Notice how Paul must defend himself before the governor of Judea, Antonius Felix. Write on a sheet of paper the main points of his defense.

Working Ahead

Complete one or more of the following before the next session:

1. In the upcoming chapters, Paul becomes entangled in the legal system of his day. If you have somehow been involved in the judicial system, whether you have been sued, criminally tried, or merely served on a jury, be prepared to share your experiences with others in the group. How did your perspective on the system change through the experience?

2. In Paul's day, the Jewish religious leaders were often divided over whether or not there would be a resurrection from the dead. The Pharisees thought there would be, while the Sadducees believed there would be none. Paul, of course, was a strong believer in the resurrection. Can you think of any ways nature itself suggests the possibility of a resurrection? Have examples ready to share with others.

3. It was Paul's dream to reach Rome with the Gospel. Paul's arrest in Jerusalem was the beginning of a series of events that would lead him to Rome. Although he had intended to travel to the seat of the empire on one of his missionary journeys, the Lord would bring him to Rome under guard and under arrest. But he still would reach Rome. Are there any goals the Lord has accomplished for you in ways you never expected?

Did You Know That . . . ?

When the Roman commander arrested Paul, he asked the apostle, "Aren't you the Egyptian who started a revolt and led four thousand terrorists out into the desert some time ago?" (Acts 21:38) The Jewish historian, Josephus, refers to this event in his writing. He records the existence of an Egyptian false prophet who led thousands of followers to the Mount of Olives. The uprising occurred some years before Paul's arrival in Jerusalem. Naturally, Roman soldiers quashed this rebellion, killing hundreds of people before the revolt came to an end. Interestingly, the leader of the movement escaped. So it was not surprising the Roman commander would wonder whether Paul, promoting some kind of religion that was causing tremendous commotion, was this same rebel!

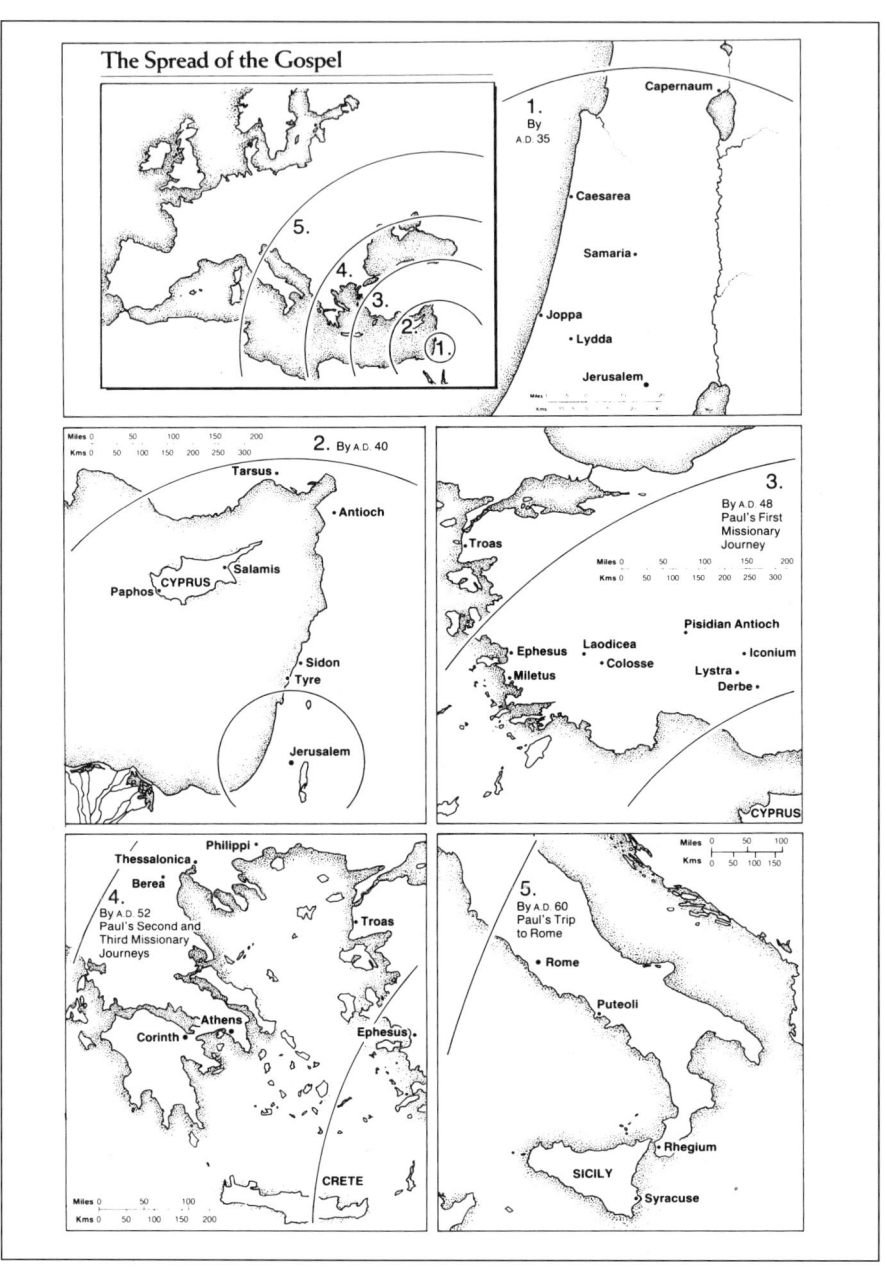

Taken from **NIV STUDY BIBLE**. Copyright © 1986 by The Zondervan Corporation. Used by permission of Zondervan Publishing House.

Session 10

The Trials Begin

Acts 23–24

Approaching This Study

Paul's arrival in Jerusalem signals the beginning of the end of the Acts narrative. In Jerusalem, another riot results from his presence, so the local Roman commander takes Paul into protective custody. In order to protect Paul from a life-threatening plot, the Roman commander arranges for Paul to journey to Caesarea. But in Caesarea, Paul, a Roman citizen, appeals to Caesar for judgment, which requires Paul's presence in Rome. He endures a shipwreck near the island of Malta but, finally, he arrives in Rome. While under house arrest, he continues to preach the Gospel of Jesus Christ to all who would listen. We never learn about the outcome of Paul's trial—at least not in the record of Acts. But, from the account, we gain an ongoing understanding of the Spirit's guidance of Christ's church. Through such individuals as Paul, the Gospel of Jesus Christ would continue to be carried to the world.

We begin to question why anyone would suffer so much simply to ensure that others would hear about the grace and forgiveness of Jesus Christ. Paul, as well as the other disciples, was a true believer in the resurrection of Jesus whose motivation for witnessing was the joy that came from knowing Jesus as Lord and Savior. They wanted others to know the joy of eternal life granted through faith in Jesus' death and resurrection.

There is much to admire in Paul's courageous defense against the Sanhedrin and the governor of Judea. He truly understood Jesus' promise in Mark 13:9, "You will be handed over to the local councils and flogged in the synagogues. On account of Me you will stand before governors and kings as witnesses to them." But Paul did not fear. He trusted in Jesus' other promise (Matthew 10:19–20): "When they arrest you, do not worry about what to say or how to say it. At that time you will be given what to say, for it will not be you speaking, but the Spirit of your Father speaking through you." And so, forewarned by Jesus and forearmed by the Spirit's power, Paul boldly confronted his fate.

In this session we will witness the Holy Spirit providing Paul with the exact words required to impact his audience and judges, providing the best opportunities for the Spirit to transform pagan hearts into faithful ones. Even though Paul's answers bring him greater turmoil, each opportunity allows the Spirit access to more souls, leading them to faith in the Lord as their Savior. And, after all, that is the prize that motivated and inspired Paul.

An Overview

Unit Reading

Silently read Acts 23–24. Jot down the highlights of the chapters.

The Message in Brief

Paul has been brought before the Sanhedrin (the ruling religious authorities in Jerusalem) so that the Roman commander can determine what offense Paul has committed. Standing before this body, Paul begins his defense. His proclamation of the resurrection brings an immediate division within the Sanhedrin, but the Pharisees, who also believe in a resurrection, defend Paul. Nevertheless, 40 of the Jews conspire to kill him, and when Paul's nephew overhears the plot, he informs the Roman commander. The commander, in turn, ensures Paul's safety by sending him to Caesarea with an escort of armed guards where he will be tried by the Roman governor, Felix. Several days later, the Jews prosecute Paul before the governor. Paul denies he is a troublemaker, claiming he worships the God of Israel and His Son Jesus. He points to the Jews from the province of Asia as the real rabble-rousers. But Felix makes no judgment. He hopes to gain a bribe from Paul; but, since no bribe arrives, Felix simply ignores the case and Paul languishes for two years in prison.

Working with the Text

The Trial before the Sanhedrin (Acts 23:1–11)

1. Paul is rebuked for insulting the high priest, Ananias. Then Paul claims he "did not realize that he was the high priest." This seems an odd statement for someone as steeped in Judaism as Paul. Can you think of any reason Paul might say this? When Paul learns he has insulted the high priest, to what wrong does he admit? How does Paul support his feelings about authority in Romans 13:1–7?

2. Why did Paul cause such a furor by simply saying to the Sanhedrin that he believed in the resurrection of the dead? Look up "Sadducees" and "Pharisees" in a Bible dictionary. How did these two groups differ?

3. How did Paul become inspired to remain courageous in his testimony about Jesus, realizing someday he would testify about Jesus in Rome as well?

The Plot against Paul Leads Him to Caesarea (Acts 23:12–35)

1. How many Jews plotted to ambush and kill Paul? How were they going to accomplish this dreadful deed? Who overheard their plans and informed the Roman commander?

2. How many men escorted Paul to Caesarea? What does this suggest to you about the commander's desire to protect Paul, the Roman citizen, until he could be fairly judged?

The Trial before the Governor (Acts 24)

1. With Paul protected in Caesarea, some of the Jews from Jerusalem were invited to bring charges against the apostle. One of them was the high priest. Who did the high priest Ananias bring with him? With what tactic did the lawyer begin his opening statements?

2. Notice how the lawyer, Tertullus, referred to the governor as "most excellent Felix." Later on, when Festus became governor, how did Paul refer to him (Acts 26:25)? When the Roman commander wrote to Felix, how was the governor addressed (Acts 23:26)? Now look at the beginning of the Gospel of Luke (Luke 1:3), which, of course, is only the first part of the two-part story extended by Luke into Acts. How did Luke address Theophilus? What does this suggest about Theophilus? And what might this imply about the reason for Luke's Gospel account and his focus on Paul throughout the Book of Acts?

3. How did the lawyer, Tertullus, refer to Christianity in Acts 24:5? Why might this have been an appropriate title? The Jews accused Paul of inciting riots and desecrating the temple. How did Paul respond to these accusations? Paul calls himself a follower of "the Way." Why might this be an appropriate title for Christianity (John 14:6)? How does Paul deflect the accusation that he belongs to a "sect," that is, a religion considered unlawful to Rome?

4. Was Christianity an unknown, foreign religion to Felix? So, how did Felix treat Paul? How would you describe the conditions under which he was "imprisoned"? What was the name of Felix's wife and what religion did she uphold? How might this help explain why Felix was so familiar with Christianity?

5. When Paul spoke to Felix about Christianity, what topics did he cover? Why do you think this might have caused Felix to fear? Felix frequently brought Paul into his presence in order to discuss Paul's thoughts. But did intellectual curiosity inspire these visits? What does Acts 24:26 suggest as the reason for Paul's frequent visits? When Felix was recalled to Rome, why didn't he free Paul?

Applying the Message

1. Although there may be many opportunities for Christians to witness their faith, we are rarely called upon to defend our beliefs before the leaders of our country. Under what conditions do you foresee Christianity becoming so foreign to Americans that its message evokes the same kind of curiosity displayed by Felix? Do you see any signs of this occurring today? Give examples.

2. How do you think people would perceive you if you called yourself "a follower of the Way" rather than a "Christian"? Can you think of some advantages to this? In other words, how easy is it for people in America to call themselves "Christians" without having any understanding of its real meaning?

3. Many people fear witnessing their faith. The very thought of "evangelism" makes them frightened and unsure. Some may participate in

evangelism "programs" that teach them how to express their faith. These programs may be valuable as long as they do not become excuses for remaining silent while still in training. Paul tells us that when we defend the faith, the Holy Spirit will give us the words to say. Knowing this promise, who will you tell about Jesus this week and when will you tell her or him?

Taking the Message Home

Review

Reread Acts 23–24. Where do you think Paul found the courage to boldly defend himself before the Sanhedrin and the Roman governor? Do you think Paul should have given Felix a bribe? Why or why not?

Looking Ahead

As time permits, read Acts 25–26. Notice again how events are leading Paul to Rome. In what way do you see the Lord's hand at work?

Working Ahead

Complete one or more of the following before the next session:

1. When Festus began to examine Paul, the apostle appealed to Caesar for judgment. The emperor at that time was Nero. Look up Nero in a Bible encyclopedia and/or dictionary. Be prepared to share your findings with the group.

2. Do you remember someone rather despicable who was converted to Christianity? If so, what was your reaction to the news of her or his conversion? Did you believe it at first? What convinced you of its authenticity? How do you think many who knew about Paul's past viewed his claim to be a Christian?

3. In the next session, one judge of Paul's defense, King Agrippa, felt it was unreasonable for Paul to think he could convert Agrippa in a "short time." Do you think a person may be converted to Christianity in a moment, or must it take many months or years of preparation for faith to be born? What examples can you think of to support your answer?

Did You Know That . . . ?

The name Felix means "happy." Felix, the governor of Judea, was originally named Antonius Claudius. He was made a freedman by the Emperor Claudius and then became a favorite of Nero. He was appointed governor of Judea in A.D. 53 largely because of his sympathy for the Jews and the fact that he was married to a Jewish princess. The Jewish historian Josephus indicates Felix dealt harshly with the constant disorder disrupting Judea. A Roman historian, Tacitus, claims Felix instigated a division between the Jews and the Samaritans for personal gain and that he enjoyed cruelty and lust. Felix was replaced as governor by Festus after Felix was recalled by Rome to stand trial for misgovernment. Eventually, he was banished and lost his son in the eruption of Mt. Vesuvius (A.D. 79).

St. Paul Rescued from the Multitude by Gustave Doré

Paul said, I am a man which am a Jew of Tarsus, a city in Cilia, a citizen of no mean city: and, I beseech thee, suffer me to speak unto the people ... (Acts 21:39 KJV). From *The Doré Bible Illustrated.* By permission of Dover Publications, Inc.

Session 11

The Trials Continue

Acts 25–26

Approaching This Study

Although none of us may have to stand before the governor of our respective states and defend our belief in the resurrection of Jesus Christ, all of us are called upon daily to confess our faith. Whether at work or at school, maybe even before family members at home, we are called to witness our faith all day, every day. Being a Christian is not something reserved for Sunday morning. It involves an entire lifestyle carried on with humility under the cross of Christ. True belief in the resurrection of Jesus Christ and the hope of eternal life will necessarily change our outlook on our everyday world. It will lead us to view all things on earth as transitory, and it will impact our desire to help others carry the burden of their own temporal journeys.

The apostle Paul experienced this transformation. He recognized that all aspects of his life must be subservient to the will of God. And, knowing he had the sure guarantee of eternal life through Jesus' death and resurrection, he boldly proclaimed the salvation of God through Jesus wherever he went—even before kings and governors. One day he would give up his very life for the sake of the Gospel. But Paul had a perfect understanding that the sufferings of this world were insignificant to the joys awaiting us in heaven. "For to me, to live is Christ and to die is gain," he once wrote. Although his earthly life had been enriched by a knowledge of Jesus Christ, although he had been so touched by the Lord that he now understood true forgiveness and peace with God, nothing would compare to the glory of seeing the Lord face to face. Knowing that Paul carried this complete and unswerving conviction, we observe him facing the new governor of Judea, Festus, and the newest Herod, Agrippa II. God would be with him, and God's Spirit would give him the right words to defend his Lord. May the Holy Spirit empower us to do the same!

An Overview

Unit Reading

Break the reading into parts. Select someone to be the narrator, another to read the voice of Paul, and another the voice of Jesus. Another volunteer should read Festus's words and another King Agrippa's.

The Message in Brief

Once Felix is replaced by Festus as governor of Judea, Paul's trials begin again. Festus wants to bring Paul back to Jerusalem so that the Jews can bring their charges against him, but Paul appeals again to Caesar in Rome. So Festus promises Paul will be sent to Rome for trial. In the meantime, Herod Agrippa II arrives to visit with Festus, and Festus explains the situation concerning Paul and the Jews. Herod's curiosity is aroused and he wants to hear for himself the charges against Paul. Paul argues he is not supporting some new and dangerous cult but is only preaching the fulfillment of Judaism. Agrippa believes Paul is hoping to convert him but finds nothing seriously wrong with Paul's preaching. Festus believes Paul has gone insane. Nevertheless, both agree Paul could have been released had he not appealed to Caesar. Paul must go to Rome.

Working with the Text

Paul's Trial before Festus (Acts 25:1–22)

1. Only three days after arriving in the province over which he would replace Felix as governor, Festus traveled to Jerusalem, curious about the charges against Paul. What did the Jews want Festus to do with Paul? Why? What did Festus agree to do?

2. How long did Festus remain with the Jews in Jerusalem before returning to Caesarea? Once he returned to Caesarea, how long was it before Paul was brought before the governor and charged? What does this suggest about the priority this case held with the governor?

3. "King Agrippa" refers to Herod Agrippa II. He was the son of the Herod who appeared in royal, dazzling robes, accepting the crowd's declaration that he was a god (remember?). As a result, God struck him dead (Acts 12:20–23). Herod Agrippa II was only 17 years old when his father died; and, although he was rather powerless at first, his territorial authority in Rome had increased considerably over the years. He would be the last of the Herods, dying around A.D. 100. Who accompanied Agrippa to Caesarea? What was her name? Why did Herod and Bernice go to Caesarea?

4. Did Festus believe the charges against Paul were very serious? How did Festus understand the argument according to his summary in Acts 25:19? Since Festus thought the dispute might reasonably be settled, he suggested Paul be escorted to the seat of his accusers in Jerusalem. But what did Paul do (Acts 25:21)?

5. After hearing about Paul's claims, how did Agrippa demonstrate his curiosity? What did Agrippa request of Festus in Acts 25:22? Look up Luke 23:8–12. How had Agrippa's great uncle demonstrated the same kind of curiosity when confronting Jesus? And how did Agrippa's great-grandfather show similar curiosity about the baby Jesus in Matthew 2:1–8?

Paul's Trial before Agrippa (Acts 25:23–26:32)

1. When Agrippa and Bernice interviewed Paul, how did they enter the audience room? Would this have intimidated you? Did it intimidate

Paul? Herod Agrippa supervised the temple treasury in Jerusalem, and he had the power to appoint the high priest. He was even consulted by Rome when it came to religious matters concerning the Jews. Why did Festus say he had brought Paul in for an interview?

2. What sect of Judaism did Paul belong to before he was converted to Christianity (Acts 26:5)? What role does Paul admit he played in the martyrdom of some of the early Christians?

3. Once again, this time in front of Festus, Paul described his vision of Jesus on the road to Damascus. What new details do we learn as Paul recounts his experience (cf. Acts 22:6–11 and Acts 9:1–9)?

4. Paul summarized his preaching by saying believers should "turn to God and prove their repentance by their deeds" (Acts 26:20). Is it deeds that save people? What is the purpose of these deeds? How does this help us understand James 2:14–24?

5. In Acts 26:22–23, Paul tried to prove he was a true Jew and not a participant in some new, outlawed sect. How did his argument insist he was only following the teachings of Moses and the prophets? What does this suggest about all believers in Jesus? How are we the "true Jews"?

6. After hearing Paul, what did Festus believe about his mental state? But what did Festus admit about Paul's knowledge?

7. What did Agrippa believe Paul was attempting to accomplish through his defense? Did Paul deny it? What does this suggest about Paul's ongoing attempts to bring the Gospel to all people?

What judgment did Festus, Agrippa, and Bernice make about Paul?

Applying the Message

1. When Festus talked to Agrippa about the problems he was having with the Jews and Paul, he said, "They had some points of dispute with him about their own religion and about a dead man named Jesus who Paul claimed was alive." That's exactly what Christians believe about Jesus. Jesus was a dead man who came alive. And this is the heart of the Christian faith. Do you know of any other religion that claims its founder was physically dead and returned physically alive to direct His followers to heaven? Why might this be a unique evangelism point for those who find it difficult to distinguish one religion from another? In other words, do you think Christian evangelism should primarily be a matter of teaching people about right and wrong, or should it focus on Jesus' death and resurrection? Why?

2. To Agrippa, Paul admitted he was once obsessed with destroying Christianity. He persecuted Christians, imprisoned them, and tried to

make them blaspheme the name of the Lord. Are you aware of any nations or people equally obsessed with destroying Christianity today? Why do you think Christianity evokes such fear and hatred in some parts of the world?

3. Look up "Diet of Worms" in an encyclopedia (it might be listed, "Worms, Diet of"). No, this is not a new and horrid method of losing weight. It is an event in history. Read through the encyclopedia's description of this event. In what ways do you see parallels between Paul's stand before Festus and Agrippa and Martin Luther's confrontation with Emperor Charles V?

Taking the Message Home

Review

Read again Acts 25 and 26 and write on a piece of paper three different qualities about Paul you have learned to admire and three which you might dislike. Do you think you could have been Paul's friend? Why?

Looking Ahead

Finish the Book of Acts by reading chapters 27–28. Notice how the ending is full of action and adventure, leading Paul to Rome—finally. If you were to write Paul's epitaph, what would it be?

Working Ahead

Complete one or more of the following before the next session:

1. Have you ever endured a dangerous experience? Write what happened and how you felt about the adventure. Did you pray to the Lord for guidance and help? How did you finally find safety?

2. In some parts of the country, certain fundamentalist sects advocate "snake-handling." Once individuals feel they have been filled with the Spirit, they handle poisonous snakes. Many are bitten, but few ill effects are noticeable. Paul was once bitten by a poisonous snake but was miraculously delivered from any illness. Do you think it's necessary for Christians to "prove" their spiritual strength and faith by performing such deeds? Why or why not?

3. Look up the island of Malta in an encyclopedia or on the Internet and discover some background information about the island on which Paul was shipwrecked. Be prepared to share your findings at the next session.

Did You Know That . . . ?

Do you remember the name of the woman who accompanied Herod Agrippa II to Caesarea? Her name was Bernice, and one might assume she was Herod's wife. Actually, she was his sister!

Bernice was the oldest daughter in the family and was one year younger than her brother. She married her uncle, Herod of Chalcis, when she was only 13 years old, bearing two children by him. But when her husband died, she began living again with her brother. Some believed they were living in incest. To counteract the gossip, she married the king of Cilicia, Polemon, but soon left him to live again with her brother. Later, she became a mistress to the Emperor Vespasian's son, Titus, but was soon ignored by him. What a sad life this privileged woman experienced!

Session 12

Sailing to Rome

Acts 27–28

Approaching This Study

The last chapters of Acts are perhaps the most adventurous of all. Paul wanted to appeal his trial in Rome because, by doing so, he was assured of reaching one important area he had not yet visited, piercing the very heart of the Roman Empire with Jesus' saving words. Throughout Paul's difficult journey to Rome, the hand of God was always present, protecting Paul and those who accompanied him through storm and shipwreck.

In these last chapters of Acts, we encounter a variety of characters, from the generous and hospitable chief official on the island of Malta, to the compassionate centurion, Julius. We witness the cowardice of the sailors who nearly abandoned ship during a couple of perilous occasions. We encounter the Christians at Sidon who helped Paul with supplies and the enthusiastic Christians of Rome who greeted Paul far outside the city limits and accompanied him to his place of house arrest. And, of course, we witness Paul's fellow Jews, some of whom heard the Gospel of Jesus Christ and received Him as their Savior and Lord, while others rejected His sacrificial death for their sins and remained blind to the saving Word. Throughout it all, we see God's church growing, and we marvel at His ongoing work through Paul and his peers.

It is likely that Paul was released from this first Roman imprisonment and reached his goal of preaching to the Gentiles in Spain. This was his expressed hope because he always believed his ministry was to carry the news about Jesus to people who had never heard of Him. As we continue to read about Paul's desire to spread the Good News of Jesus' death and resurrection throughout the empire, we are reminded that, as a result of his hard and courageous work among the Gentiles, Christianity is not some local Palestinian religion but a faith upheld by people around the world.

We can approach this last session of our study by considering how contemporary missionaries continue the endeavor begun by Paul so many years ago, bringing the Gospel of Jesus to places, tribes, and people who have not yet heard. Although these missionaries are not any of the original apostles of the Lord, the message they carry is the same proclaimed by Paul so many years ago. Through this message the Holy Spirit continues to deliver people from sin, death, and the devil!

An Overview

Unit Reading

Acts 27–28 is a narrative of Paul's final travels before reaching Rome and his attempts to reach many of the Jews in Rome with the Gospel. Have volunteers read aloud both chapters.

The Message in Brief

Because Paul had appealed to Caesar, he had to be escorted to the Roman capital for trial. He is placed, along with other prisoners and soldiers, on a ship supervised by a centurion named Julius. As they sail towards Crete, they encounter a devastating storm that threatens their lives for two weeks, terrifying all aboard. The storm dumps them on the coast of Malta, and all aboard are spared disaster because Paul is present. On Malta, Paul is bitten by a poisonous snake but shows no reaction. This amazes the residents of the island and they bring their sick to him to heal. After spending the winter on the island, Paul and the others continue their journey to Rome. Paul is greeted by the Christians in Rome and placed under house arrest. From his rented house, he is able to preach to many Jews about Jesus Christ. Some believe and some do not. But for two years he continues sharing the Gospel of Jesus Christ to all who will listen.

Working with the Text

Paul Sails for Rome and Encounters a Storm (Acts 27:1–26)

1. According to Acts 27:1, who was with Paul once again? What was the name of the centurion who was in charge of the prisoners? We know nothing about this man; but, because he allowed Paul to go to his friends in Sidon for personal supplies (Acts 27:3), he seems to have been a com-

passionate centurion. As we read about Paul's journey to Rome, it might be useful to refer to a Bible atlas and pinpoint the various ports and islands through which he passes.

2. Sailing became dangerous "after the Fast" (Acts 27:9). Luke, the writer, would be referring to the Day of Atonement that Jews observed during the latter part of September or in October. The Romans thought it was very dangerous to sail across the Mediterranean after September 15. And after November 11, it was considered deadly. What warning did Paul give the sailors of the Alexandrian ship? But what did Julius, the owner of the ship, and the pilot decide?

3. Paul and his shipmates were sailing on the eastern side of Crete when a "northeaster" arose. The "northeaster" was a gale-force wind that came sweeping down from the northeast (obviously!) and carried the ship away from Crete into the middle of the Mediterranean. The ship had a lifeboat tied behind it. What did the shipmates do with the lifeboat as they were blown to sea? Everyone feared the ship would be torn apart and they would be drowned. What did they begin to do, hoping to make the ship lighter and harder to sink? Paul finally had good news—and bad news—for all aboard. What was it?

Paul Suffers a Shipwreck at Malta (Acts 27:27–28:10)

1. For two weeks, the ship was blown about the sea. When the sailors felt they were nearing the shore in the middle of the night, how did they determine their proximity to land? What cowardly act did some of the sailors attempt? What stopped them from fleeing?

2. For two weeks, very little food was eaten because all aboard were terrified. What did Paul ask them to do? Describe how he began the meal. How many mouths were on board? And what did they do with the remaining food?

3. They attempted to beach the ship in an unknown bay in a strange land. Describe how they attempted this process and what resulted.

4. When their plans went awry, what did the soldiers plan to do with the prisoners? Why does this make grisly sense? How did Julius again show his compassion for Paul and the other prisoners? By what two methods did the ship's passengers, soldiers, and sailors make it safely to shore?

5. How would you describe the islanders on Malta? Were they shy and introverted or friendly and outgoing? How did they demonstrate these traits? What miracle bedazzled the islanders? How was the miracle a fulfillment of Jesus' promise in Mark 16:18? How did the islanders view Paul after this miracle? Compare their reactions to those demonstrated by the Lystrans in Acts 14:11–18. What did Paul do for Publius's father and all the other sick on the island?

Paul Reaches Rome (Acts 28:11–31)

1. Paul and everyone else wintered on the island of Malta. Only by late February or early March was it safe to sail once again. Look up "Castor and Pollux" in an encyclopedia. Why were these two figures appropriate to place on a ship?

2. What did the Christians in Rome do when Paul approached their city? Why would this be so heartening? What happened to Paul when he arrived in Rome? Paul was able to gain the ears of the Jews in Rome and speak to them. What was his argument? How did the Jews respond? What writings did Paul use to convince the Jews that Jesus was the long-awaited Messiah? How successful was Paul?

3. How long did Paul continue to meet with all who would listen in Rome? What do you think about the ending to Acts? Is it satisfying? What do you think should have been added to complete the story?

Applying the Message

1. After reading these last two chapters of Acts, how important was it for Luke to record events in a factual manner? Now, remember that the same author of Acts wrote the Gospel of Luke. Read Luke's account of the resurrection and Jesus' appearance to the disciples in Luke 24:1–12, 36–48. How does this understanding of the author's intent strengthen the reality of the resurrection account?

2. When Paul convinced his shipmates to eat some food after they had abstained for nearly two weeks, he gave thanks to God "in front of them all." Do you think it is important for Christians not only to give thanks to God before meals at home but also in restaurants and at other people's homes? How might this witness their faith?

3. After completing the Book of Acts, what do you think about Paul? How would you like to imitate him? Are there some characteristics you could do without? Why? List those characteristics you admire most about Paul.

Taking the Message Home

Review

Read through these two last chapters of Acts with your Bible atlas nearby. Once again, trace the journey that led Paul from Caesarea to Rome. What was the most exciting moment of this last adventure?

Looking Ahead

Spend some time reflecting on the incredible story you just read. Ponder the power and presence of the Holy Spirit in the early church. Consider the heroism of Paul and the other disciples as they sacrificed their very lives for the sake of the Gospel. And reflect on the willingness of God to intervene whenever His will was in danger of being thwarted. How do these thoughts reshape your vision of the Christian church today?

Working Ahead

Use the following for further study:

1. Read Paul's last existing letter, 2 Timothy. Can you tell Paul was suffering from a far more serious imprisonment than the one described in Acts? See 2 Timothy 1:16–17; 2:9; 4:13–18. What can you tell about his mood?

2. Read Paul's letter to Titus. Are there any names mentioned in the epistle that refer to people described by Luke in Acts? Who are they?

3. Find a church history book and learn a little bit more about how early Christianity spread and flourished throughout the known world.

Did You Know That . . . ?

What happened to Paul after the end of Acts? There are a number of compelling reasons to believe he was released from prison and began another missionary journey. For example, some of Paul's letters were written from this Roman imprisonment, and a couple of these letters express his hope to visit the other churches very soon. He must have been looking forward to an imminent release (Philippians 2:24; Philemon 22). Some of Paul's letters (1, 2 Timothy and Titus) refer to experiences that Acts does not record, suggesting these events occurred at a later time. Furthermore, tradition claims Paul traveled to Spain on his last missionary journey. A fourth century Christian bishop and historian states Paul was finally martyred under Nero's persecution in A.D. 67.

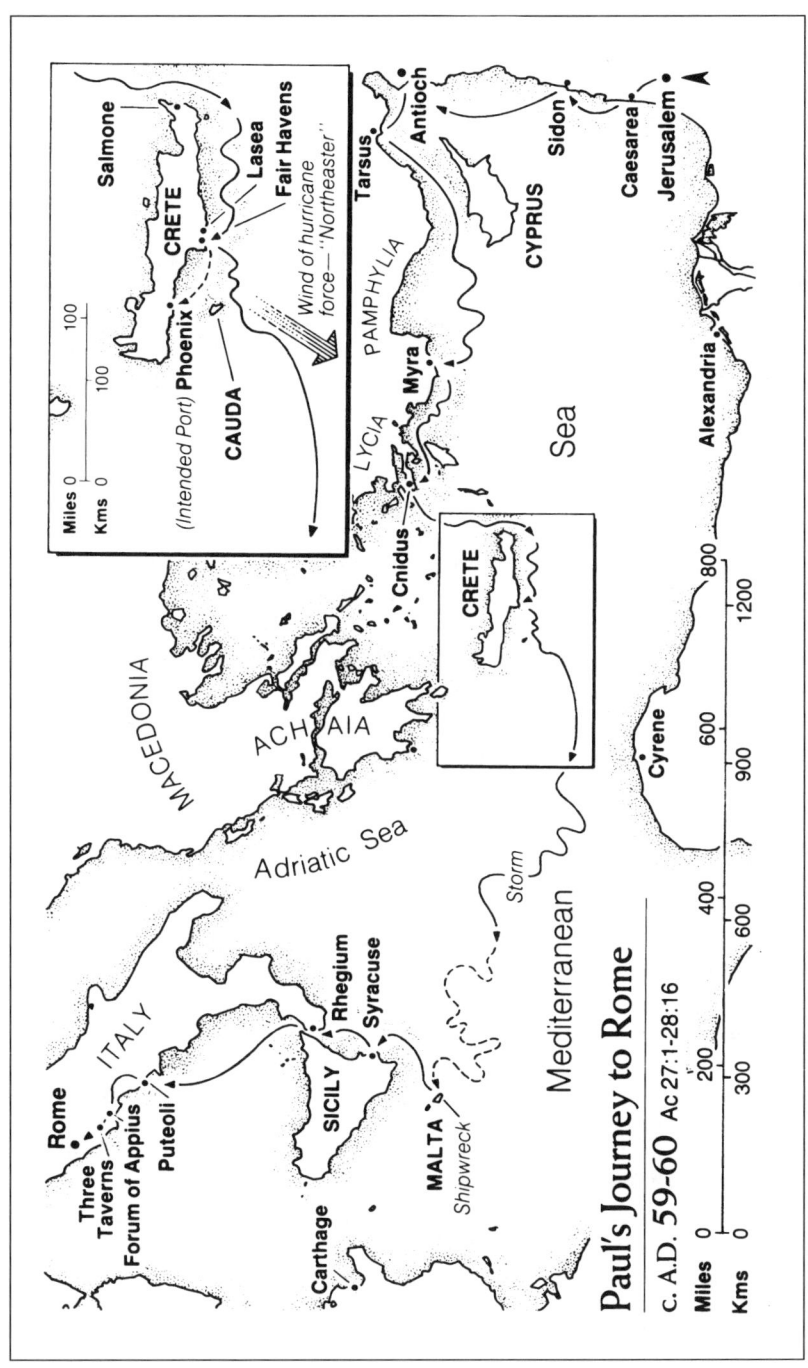

Taken from **NIV STUDY BIBLE**. Copyright © 1986 by The Zondervan Corporation. Used by permission of Zondervan Publishing House.

Glossary

adultery. Consensual sexual intercourse between a person and another person's spouse. Jesus interprets the Sixth Commandment, which forbids adultery, as forbidding all kinds of sexual indecency in both deed and thought (Matthew 5:28).

amen. The word *amen* is spoken when one wants to express "so be it." It indicates confirmation or agreement.

angels. Literally "messengers." Most often used for spiritual, heavenly beings who were created by God. Some angels, led by Satan, rebelled against God. Holy angels, who did not rebel, continually do God's bidding. They protect and serve people who have faith in God. Angels differ in rank.

anoint. To apply oil to a person or thing. Sometimes anointing was simply a part of grooming. After washing or bathing, people anointed themselves. Hosts anointed their guests as an act of courtesy or respect. Anointing was also done at a person's induction into the office of priest, king, or sometimes prophet to indicate that the person was being set apart for that particular service. Christ was anointed with the Holy Spirit.

Antichrist. One who is both an enemy of Christ and a usurper of His rights and names.

apocalyptic literature. A type of literature that is highly symbolic and deals with the revelation of mysteries, especially concerning the end times. Biblical examples of this type of literature include Daniel 7–12 and Revelation. Apocalyptic literature, usually written in times of oppression, was primarily meant to encourage God's people.

apostles. Used several times in a general sense to mean "messengers," in the New Testament this word most often refers to those who were specifically commissioned by Jesus to proclaim the Gospel. Most prominent of the apostles were the Twelve and Paul. The teaching of the apostles, along with that of the prophets, is the foundation of the church. *See also* disciples.

Baptism. Christian Baptism, the application of water in the name of the triune God—Father, Son, and Holy Spirit—is a sacrament. The way the water is applied to the individual can vary. The New Testament makes no distinction between adult and infant Baptism. Christian Baptism works the forgiveness of sins; it delivers one from spiritual death and the devil; it gives eternal salvation to all who believe Christ; it confers the Holy Spirit. Baptism also makes one a member of the body of Christ, the church. *See also* sacrament.

Bethlehem. The birthplace of Jesus Christ, thus fulfilling the Old Testament prophecy found in Micah 5:2.

Capernaum. The center of Jesus' Galilean ministry. The site of some of His early miracles and the calling of some of His disciples.

Christ. Greek for the Hebrew word *Messiah,* which means "Anointed One." Throughout the Old Testament, God promised to send the Messiah to deliver His people from their enemies and to set up His kingdom. Jesus is that Messiah.

church. The collective gathering of God's people. The New Testament speaks of the church both as the Christians gathered in a specific place and as all Christians everywhere of all time. It is also described as the fellowship of God's people, the bride of Christ, the body of Christ, and a building of which Jesus Christ is the chief cornerstone.

circumcision. Removal of the foreskin of the penis. Circumcision was a stipulation of the covenant God made with Abraham and his descendants. It showed that He would be their God, and they were to belong to Him. Controversy erupted in the early Christian church about whether Gentile Christians needed to be circumcised. St. Paul spoke God's Word to this controversy when he declared that circumcision was not required of Gentiles who became Christians.

congregation. An assembly of people gathered for worship and religious instruction; a collective, religious group.

conversion. An act of God's grace by which a sinful person is turned around and brought into God's kingdom. Conversion is accomplished by the Holy Spirit, who brings the person to faith in Christ through the Word.

covenant. An agreement between two or more tribes, nations, or individuals in which one or all of the parties promise under oath to do or refrain from doing something. Scripture records a number of covenants God has made with His people.

deacon. Someone who serves. In the early church, deacons were chosen to relieve the apostles of caring for the physical needs of widows and other poor people.

demons. Evil spirits who are against God and His work. They are angels who rebelled against God and now follow Satan.

disciples. Students or learners. In the New Testament *disciples* most often refers to Jesus' followers. Sometimes it refers specifically to the Twelve, but often it applies to a larger group of those who followed Jesus and learned from His teaching. *See also* apostles.

doctrine. Instruction or teaching; a body of beliefs about such theological issues as God, Christ, humanity, the church, and salvation.

Easter. Originally a pagan festival honoring a Teutonic (ancient Germanic) goddess of light and spring. By the eighth century the name was applied to the commemoration of Christ's resurrection.

elder. In the New Testament *elder* and *bishop* are both used to mean "overseer." The elder or presbyter was a man the apostles appointed in each Christian congregation to be its spiritual leader.

elect. The elect are those who have faith in Christ as the promised Messiah and Savior.

election. The doctrine that explains the biblical truth that God from eternity planned our salvation and chose by His grace those who will be saved in Christ. No one deserves to be saved. God, however, desires that all people be saved. By God's grace through faith alone in Jesus, people (the elect) are saved. Those who have received God's gift of faith respond in thankfulness to God for His love and grace in choosing them.

epistle. A formal letter; one of the letters adopted as books of the New Testament.

eternal life. Abiding fellowship with God of infinite duration. Eternal life begins when the Holy Spirit by grace brings a person to faith in Jesus Christ. Although the Christian already has eternal life, he or she will not experience it fully until the resurrection of the dead and the life of the world to come.

faith. The belief and trust in the promise of God in Christ Jesus, worked by the Holy Spirit, through which a person is brought into a right relationship with God and saved. The Holy Spirit works faith in Christ in the individual through Word and Sacrament.

fellowship. Sharing something in common. By grace, through faith in Christ, God has given believers fellowship, that is, an intimate relationship, with Himself. Through the work of the Holy Spirit, fellow believers also have a oneness in Christ and share with one another the common bond of the Gospel and faith in Christ.

forgiveness. God's act whereby He ends the separation caused by peoples' sins and restores people to a proper relationship with Him. Forgiveness is a gift of God, given out of grace for Christ's sake. As a result of Christ's forgiveness, we are to forgive our neighbor. Recognizing that we are sinful and being sorry for our sins precedes forgiveness.

Gentiles. Non-Hebrew peoples of the world; people outside the Jewish faith.

glory. That which shows the greatness of someone or something. The glory of God is shown in and by His great miracles, His eternal perfection, His creation, and all His works. Most importantly, it is shown by His Son, our Lord Jesus Christ, and the salvation He won for all people.

Gnosticism. A belief system that reached its peak in the second and third centuries A.D. According to the Gnostics, salvation came by hating the world and everything physical and by escaping to the spirit world through special knowledge. Gnostics said Jesus came not to save people from sin but to show them how to escape to the spiritual world.

Gospel (Good News). The message that Jesus Christ has fulfilled the Law for all people and paid the penalty for their sin on the cross, thus having won forgiveness and salvation for them.

gospels. The first four books of the New Testament. Matthew, Mark, Luke, and John each wrote one of the books. They are called gospels because they tell the good news of how salvation was won for all people by Jesus Christ.

grace. God's undeserved love and favor revealed in Jesus Christ by which He is moved to forgive people's sins and grant them salvation. Grace is a quality within God. It is also referred to as God's steadfast love or faithfulness.

heaven. The invisible world or universe from which God rules; the home of angels. Christ rules from heaven and receives believers there. *See also* paradise.

heir. The individual to whom another person's wealth or possessions, the person's inheritance, is given after the person dies.

hell. The place of eternal punishment.

heresy. Stubborn error in an article of faith in opposition to Scripture.

holy. An essential aspect of God's nature, holiness is the state of being without sin. Those who trust in Christ for salvation have been declared holy and righteous in God's sight. The Holy Spirit through the Gospel works in believers to motivate and empower them to lead lives of holiness. *Holy* can also be used to refer to something set apart to be used for or by God.

hymn. A song telling about God and praising Him.

inspiration. The special way the Holy Spirit worked in certain people to cause them to act out, speak, or write God's Word. When the Holy Spirit did this, the person who was inspired was certainly under the direction of God's power, but he or she was not a robot. Thus, as Paul says, "All Scripture is God-breathed" (2 Timothy 3:16).

Israel. (1) The name given to Jacob after he wrestled with God (Genesis 32:28). (2) The name of the nation composed of the descendants of Jacob and his 12 sons. Jacob and his sons founded the 12 tribes of Israel. (3) The name given to the 10 northern tribes of Israel after Solomon's death, when they revolted against Rehoboam and the kingdom split in two. The Northern Kingdom was called Israel to distinguish it from the Southern Kingdom, which was called Judah. (4) *Israel* is also used to describe all who follow in the faith of Abraham, Isaac, and Jacob and, therefore, are true Israelites, no matter what their physical descent.

Jerusalem. The state and religious capital of the Hebrew nation. Jesus was arrested, tried, and crucified in Jerusalem.

Jesus. Greek for the Hebrew name *Joshua,* which means "Yahweh (the Lord) saves."

Jew. A later derivation of the word *Judean,* which referred to someone who belonged to the tribe or kingdom of Judah as opposed to people in the Northern Kingdom. *Hebrew* (derived from Eber; Genesis 10:21–25) denotes those who descended from Abraham through Isaac and Jacob; *Israel* denotes those who descended from Jacob; and *Judean,* later *Jew,* denotes those who descended from the tribe or kingdom of Judah. As well as being an ethnic designation, the term *Jew* also refers to the adherents of a religion. While in New Testament times some Jews were faithful adherents of the faith of the Old Testament, others had begun to deviate from that faith. During the time between the Old and New Testaments, a number of Jewish religious groups had developed, such as the Pharisees and the Sadducees. The pharisaic branch survived after New Testament times and has most influenced the religion called Judaism, a combination of oral tradition with the Old Testament. *See* Pharisees.

Jordan River. Connects the Sea of Galilee to the Dead Sea. It is the river in which Jesus was baptized by John.

Judah. (1) The fourth son of Jacob and Leah. Jacob bestowed the blessing of the birthright on Judah. Jesus was one of Judah's descendants. (2) The tribe that descended from Judah. It occupied the greater part of southern Palestine. (3) The kingdom of Judah that began when the 10 northern tribes withdrew from Rehoboam around 930 B.C. The kingdom of Judah lasted until 587 B.C., when Jerusalem fell to the Babylonians. The kingdom of Judah existed in the southern part of Palestine.

justification. The gracious act of God by which He pronounces people to be not guilty of their sin through faith in Jesus. The basis for His acquittal is that Jesus Christ fulfilled the Law in humanity's place and paid the penalty for all people's sin by His suffering and death on the cross.

kingdom of God. A spiritual kingdom, ruled by God, that includes people from all nations. The New Testament sometimes pictures God's kingdom as the rule of the Holy Spirit in the hearts of God's people. The kingdom of God is, at times, spoken of as a future blessing, as in the kingdom Jesus will bring on the Last Day, and, at times, as a present reality. The church proclaims the kingdom of God by preaching the Gospel.

Lord. (1) LORD (printed in capital and small capital letters) is the way Yahweh, God's personal name in the Old Testament, is often rendered in English. (2) Lord (capital *L* and the remaining letters lowercase) translates the Hebrew word *adon*. It means "master" and denotes ownership. (3) At some point, probably after the exile, God's people stopped pronouncing *Yahweh* and instead said *Adonai* whenever they saw the consonants for Yahweh (YHWH) in the Hebrew Bible. (4) The Greek word *kyrios* is also translated as Lord. It is the word used for a human master or for God as ruler. It is also used for Christ.

Lord's Supper. Christ instituted this supper on the night of His betrayal. It is to be celebrated in the church until His return as a proclamation of His death for the sins of the world. In this meal Christ gives His body and blood in, with, and under the bread and wine. Christians who trust in the blessings Christ promises to give in this meal and partake of it in faith receive forgiveness of sins, life, salvation, and a strengthening of their faith. Also called "Breaking of Bread," "Holy Communion," "Eucharist," and "the Lord's Table."

love. Various types of love are referred to in the Bible. The Greek word *agape* represents God's love for sinful people. This is the kind of love Christians are to have.

mercy. The aspect of God's character that moves Him to spare or help those in distress. As Christians have been shown mercy by God, they are to be merciful to others.

Messiah. Hebrew for "Anointed One." *See* Christ.

minister. A person who has been called—by God, through the church—to spiritually feed and care for God's people. All Christians have vocations—callings by God in life. All Christians have received various gifts of the Holy Spirit for the building up of others in the church. All Christians are members of the priesthood of all believers (1 Peter 2:9). However, ministers have a distinct calling from God, even as Jesus chose 12 of His disciples to serve as apostles.

miracle. An event that causes wonder; something that takes place outside of the laws of nature. The New Testament depicts miracles as acts of power, signs, and wonders. Their significance could be understood only by those who had faith in Jesus Christ.

Nazareth. Jesus' hometown. The place where He grew up after His family returned from Egypt. He was not well received in Nazareth when He returned during His ministry.

ordination. A rite (act) of the church by which the church, through a congregation, publicly confers the pastoral office on a qualified man. Ordination has its historical roots in the New Testament and in the early church. In the New Testament, deacons, missionaries, and elders were called to their offices, just as today a congregation calls a man to be its pastor.

parable. A saying or story that uses an illustration from everyday life for the purpose of teaching a moral or religious truth. An earthly story with a heavenly or spiritual meaning. Although the events and characters in the parable are true to nature, not every detail of the story has a spiritual meaning. Rather, there is only one main point of comparison. Jesus often spoke in parables to teach the people about Himself and the kingdom of heaven.

paradise. Used in the New Testament to describe heaven, the home of those who die in Christ. *See* heaven.

peace. Often used to describe that state of spiritual tranquility and harmony that God gives when He brings one into a right relationship with Himself through Christ.

Pentecost. The Jewish Feast of Weeks, which was celebrated 50 days after the offering of the barley sheaf during the Feast of Unleavened Bread. Pentecost is also known as the Feast of Harvest and the Day of Firstfruits. On this day the Holy Spirit was poured out on the disciples, and many people came to faith in Christ after hearing Peter's Spirit-filled preaching.

Pharisees. One of several Jewish religious parties in New Testament times. Economically many of them came from the middle class. They were characterized by scrupulous keeping of the mosaic Law and the oral traditions added to the Law. It was their desire to make the Law understandable and applicable so that people might fully obey it. Thus, they formulated lists of rules, spelling out exactly, for example, what constituted work on the Sabbath day. In this way they sought to build a "fence" around the Law to keep people from getting close to violating the commandments of the Law. In general, the Jews highly respected the Pharisees. No doubt many Pharisees were sincere in their beliefs, such as Nicodemus. But many others, however, fell into hypocrisy, living by the letter of the Law but having lost its spirit.

prayer. Speaking with God. Prayers can be formal or spoken freely from one's own thoughts and concerns. They can be said together by a group of believers or alone by an individual. They can be said at set times and places or in all times and places.

priests. These men served in the temple in Jerusalem on a rotational basis. There they offered sacrifices on behalf of the people and saw to other matters of temple worship. They were also to teach the Law to the people. It was required of priests that they remain ceremonially clean or pure, or else they could not perform their priestly duties. Examples of activities or things that would make a person unclean were contact with a dead body, seminal emission, and leprosy. Entering the house of a "sinner," tax collector, or Gentile was considered to make a person unclean because it would involve contact with those who did not keep themselves ritually or morally clean.

Redeemer, redemption. Redemption is the buying back of humanity from sin and death by Christ, the Redeemer, who paid the price with His perfect obedience and His sacrificial death on the cross.

repentance. A total change of heart and life that God works in an individual who does not believe or trust in Him by turning him or her around to one who does believe and trust in Him. Repentance includes both sorrow for one's sins and faith in Christ through whom forgiveness is granted.

resurrection. A return to life after one has died.

righteous. That which is right in accordance with the Law. The term is particularly used to describe people who are in a right relationship with God through faith in Christ.

sacrament. A word the church uses to describe a sacred act instituted by God where there are visible means connected to His Word. In a sacrament God offers, gives, and seals to the individual the forgiveness of sins earned by Christ.

sacrifice. An act of worship where a person presents an offering to God. God commanded sacrifices in the Old Testament as a way for sins to be atoned for and as a means for people to express thankfulness to Him. Among the main sacrifices mentioned in the Old Testament are the sin offering, the trespass offering, the burnt offering, the peace offering, and the meal and drink offerings. At other times, offerings were sacrificed on the altar in front of the tabernacle and later at the temple morning and evening, at each Sabbath and new moon, and at the three leading festivals. All sacrifices pointed to and were fulfilled in Christ, the Lamb of God, sacrificed for the sins of the world.

salvation. Deliverance from any type of evil, both physical and spiritual. Spiritual salvation includes rescue from sin. It is a gift of God's grace through faith in Christ.

Samaria. During Old Testament times the capital city of the Northern Kingdom of Israel. During New Testament times, the land of the Samaritans between Galilee in the north and Judea in the south. Interestingly, the most direct route from Nazareth to Jerusalem led directly through Samaria. Yet, most Jews would avoid that route, taking a significant detour across the Jordan River and then south.

Samaritans. The Samaritans were a mixed race of people, descended partly from the tribes of the Northern Kingdom of Israel and partly from Gentiles who were settled in Israel during the exilic period of the Old Testament. The Samaritans worshiped the God of Israel, but their religion differed from that of the Jews in significant ways. They, for example, accepted the authority of the Pentateuch only and rejected the rest of the Hebrew Scriptures. Jews and Samaritans, although culturally very similar, lived on "opposite sides of the tracks." They were often bigoted toward each other and avoided each other. Like tax collectors, Samaritans were thought by Jews to have no place in the messianic kingdom.

Satan. The chief fallen angel and enemy of God, humanity, and all that is good. Sometimes called Abaddon, Apollyon, or Beelzebul (Beelzebub).

Sea of Galilee. Jesus spent much of His early ministry around the Sea of Galilee. The sea is the place where Jesus walked on water and calmed the storm. The sea (more properly considered a lake) supported a fishing industry.

sin. Sin is both doing what God forbids and failing to do what He commands.

Because of sin everyone deserves temporal and eternal death. Only through faith in Christ, who kept God's Law perfectly and suffered the punishment for the sins of the world, does one escape the results of sin.

Son of God. A title applied to Jesus in a unique sense. It says that Jesus as the Son is equal to God the Father.

Son of Man. The term Jesus most often used to refer to Himself. One aspect of this title is that it emphasizes the power and dominion the Son of Man receives from the Ancient of Days. (See Daniel 7:9, 13–14 and Matthew 16:27.)

soul, spirit. The soul is not separate from the body; rather it is that which gives life. It animates the flesh. It is the inner person as distinguished from the flesh. The soul departs at death. It is the seat of the appetites, emotions, and passions. It can be lost and saved.

Suffering Servant. Jesus is the fulfillment of the Suffering Servant prophesied in the Old Testament (Isaiah 42:1–4; 49:1–6; 50:4–9; 52:13–53:12).

tabernacle. The tent that God commanded His people to build after He delivered them from bondage in Egypt and where He promised to dwell among them (Exodus 25:8). The tabernacle served as Israel's center of worship until Solomon's temple was built. *See also* temple.

tax collectors. These people collected taxes for the Roman Empire. Roman taxes were very high, and it was the practice of the empire to hand over the collection of taxes to individuals or businesses, who would add a certain percentage to the amount collected. Needless to say, this system, called "tax farming," was open to abuse. Most Jews hated tax collectors, viewing them as usurers and thieves who supported the godless Roman oppressors. Tax collectors were deemed unclean. They were cut off from the people of God and were thought to have no place in the messianic kingdom.

teachers of the law. Specialists in and teachers of Jewish ceremonial, civil, and moral laws.

temple. The fixed sanctuary of the Lord that replaced the tabernacle as God's dwelling place among His people. The temple was the center of Israelite and then Jewish worship until it was destroyed. *See also* tabernacle. Jesus, God who took on human flesh, replaced the temple as God's dwelling place among His people (John 1:14; 2:19–21; see also Revelation 21:22).

testament. A document outlining the distribution of a person's property after death. When the Old Testament (originally written in Hebrew and Aramaic) was translated into Greek, the Hebrew word for "covenant" was translated by the Greek word for "testament." This same Greek word is used in Jesus' Words of Institution (see Mark 14:24) and is translated by some as "covenant" and by others as "testament." *See also* covenant.

tithe. A tenth part of one's income given as an offering to the Lord. According to the mosaic law, a tenth of all produce of land and herds was sacred to the Lord.

transfiguration. The name given to the occasion when Jesus was visibly glorified in the presence of three of His disciples.

Trinity. The church's term for the coexistence of Father, Son, and Holy Spirit in the unity of the Godhead—three distinct persons in one divine being, or essence. The term *Trinity* does not occur in the Bible, but many passages support the doctrine of the Trinity.

unleavened bread. Bread made without yeast. The Israelites ate unleavened bread at Passover and the following Feast of Unleavened Bread as a reminder of the haste with which they left Egypt during the exodus. They did not have time to bake bread but took with them unleavened dough that they baked in the wilderness.

will. Inclination or choice. God's will is revealed in His acts, His Law, and especially in Christ. Although the will of fallen human beings has some capacity to perform works that conform outwardly to God's Law, humanity's fallen or natural will cannot incline itself toward God or choose to have true faith in Him. Only the Holy Spirit working through the Gospel can create in people true faith in God. *See also* works.

Word. God's Word is the means through which He makes Himself known and reveals His will to humanity. His Word is the primary way in which He works His purposes in the world. The Holy Scriptures are the written Word of God. They tell of the purpose of God in creating, saving, and sanctifying His people. They testify to Jesus Christ, the Word of God made flesh. He is the supreme revelation of God.

works. Whether a person's works are ultimately deemed good or bad in God's sight depends on that person's relationship to God. Only a person who believes in Jesus Christ as Savior can do good works in God's eyes, since good works are a fruit of faith.

world. Used in Scripture not only to describe the universe or the human race, but often to denote the wicked and unbelievers, those who are opposed to God.

worship. To bow down, kiss the hand, revere, serve. The respect and reverence given to God. New Testament worship is centered in and around the Word of God. It involves reading Scripture, singing hymns and spiritual songs, teaching, praying, and celebrating the Lord's Supper. In Christian worship God bestows His gifts of forgiveness, life, and salvation upon us through His Word and Sacraments, and we respond in thankfulness and praise.

Zealots. Members of an ultra-nationalistic first-century A.D. Jewish political group. They were similar to the Pharisees in their general beliefs, but where the Pharisees might be ready to die for their faith, the Zealots were ready to kill for it. They advocated the use of force against the Romans.